ABUNDANT JOY

A 90-DAY JOURNEY TOWARD SUSTAINABLE, AUTHENTIC, LIFE-CHANGING JOY

KRISTINA STONE KAISER

APOCRYPHILE
PRESS

Apocryphile Press
PO Box 255
Hannacroix, NY 12087
www.apocryphilepress.com

Please join our mailing list at www.apocryphilepress.com/free. We'll keep you up-to-date on all our new releases, and we'll also send you a FREE BOOK. Visit us today!

CONTENTS

INTRODUCTION

They say everyone has a breaking point, a moment when their problems and difficulties begin to feel so great that they no longer believe they can continue on as usual.

For me, that moment lasted about 4 years. It began in the Spring of 2018, crested in the summer of 2020, and slowly transformed into my "now" over the next couple of years. When I look back on it, I wonder how it didn't all come to a head sooner. I was on the doorstep of my 40th birthday, and I had been pastoring a small church in a suburb of Boston for almost a decade, a church that had come to include a community center and a film production arm. We lived our lives moving from one event to another. And in those very brief moments where we would steal away to the farm in Wisconsin, it was interesting to hear the question that emerged from our families' lips: "Why don't your kids ask to go outside?" I had to think about that one…

…By the way…speaking of the kids, we have four of them. The age gap between them spans eight years, and every single one of them is a miracle, albeit very needy miracles.

And so back to that question: Why didn't the kids ask to go

outside? Well, when I stopped to think about it, I realized it was because they had learned a different question: What are we doing today? I had built my life around trying to help others make their dreams come true. And though we weren't successful by the standards that many would have used to measure success, I often had this feeling that we were just around the corner from any number of possible breakthroughs, breakthroughs that were going to make it all worth it.

And then came the Spring of 2018, for which, the short version of the story is: In trying to be the best helper I could be, I did one of the last things I would ever want to do: I hurt my friends.

I certainly wasn't trying to hurt them. But in trying to be, be, be and do, do, do, I had put on too many hats at once, and it all came crashing down. Even as the walls of a friendship were crumbling, I very much tried to keep going. I tried to repair the relationship, I went to work as usual, I kept things running smoothly at home. But my spiritual practice notably took on this quality that merged the angst of high school poetry with the realities of a middle-aged woman.

Simply put, I was sad. But more than that, I was heartsick and exhausted. How could all of this work and effort result in an irreparably broken friendship? After limping along for almost 2 years, I entered into several years of inner work and healing, which began with a move back to central Wisconsin.

The shift in environment was both terrifying and...no, pretty much it was just terrifying. I had no idea what I would do for work. And it wasn't lost on me that we were moving far away from friends that we thought of as family and a certain amount of diversity that we knew we wouldn't be able to capture in a far more rural setting. Add to it, we were embarking on this great pilgrimage in June of 2020—in the middle of a pandemic—which meant that when we planted ourselves in our new home, not only did the furniture, clothes, and kitchen supplies not arrive for 30 days, the closest we came to meeting anyone was a plate of cookies left on the front porch with a lovely, "Welcome to the neighborhood" note.

For about a year people asked me (via Zoom, of course,) "What are you going to do?" And repeatedly, I answered with three very uncomfortable words: I don't know. When I looked 5 years into the future, there was no clear path in sight.

By the fall of 2021, however, I began training to become a certified Spiritual Guide—someone who companions others as they seek to make sense of their own story. Who are we? What are we doing? Why are we doing it? How are we doing it? What does it all mean—for today and for the long haul?

That journey became the highlight of my existence for almost 2 years as I awakened again to what was in the core of my being. Sometimes that looked both weird and beautiful all at the same time. To give you an example, I'd be at the window in our...(gonna be honest here)...bathroom, and I would say things like, "Dominic, come here! Smell the air! Do you smell that? Did you remember that Wisconsin air smells like that? Wow! Smell that air!" (Hopefully, anyone out for a late-night stroll with their dog didn't realize we were enjoying the crisp night air from our bathroom.)

I began to hear the birds—like, really hear them. I went on walks and learned what bees do when it rains. I joined a handbell choir—and became so enthusiastic about it that I think I actually weirded the others out. I'm not sure they even believed me when I would say things like, "There's no place else I'd rather be right now!" They really did look at me with that sideways-tilt-of-the-head thing as they would, first, try to match my energy, and then just decide to leave me to it.

I surrounded myself with people that gave me room to speak what felt true to me, which wasn't always easy. Not saying yes to everything has been a hard habit to break. But they gave me room to make my life be about more than goals and metrics. And through it all, I spent a little bit of time in "practice" every day.

What you will find throughout this book are little parts of the journey I've been on. These very simple, very easy-to-do practices ultimately helped me connect again to my own deepest Joy—my own inner Wellspring. In truth, we never really lose our Joy, even if we lose sight of it from time to time. And if you're like me—and I'd like to think most people are—you don't have two hours a day to sit on a cushion. You can't get up any earlier than you already are, and if you try to experience that deeper-meaning-connection at the end of the day, it's going to result in falling asleep and feeling like a failure. We need practices that fit into our lives and that are easy to do from wherever we are.

The practices on these pages helped me do just that. They helped me learn to incorporate Joy even in the midst of the difficulties of my life. And that is a very real part of it. This 90-day Journey is not about creating a perfect life. It's about how our experience of life changes when we learn to hold space for the whole of our lives, when we have had tangible practice incorporating those things that return us to Joy more readily.

As I have learned how to regularly invest in Joy, the result has been a return to balance. It doesn't mean I'm never upset. It means that when I am upset, I can allow myself to feel that way. And, I can also remain connected to that which is life-giving and sustains me beyond my uncertainties and disappointments.

My hope is that this 90-day Journey will bring you back to your own inner Wellspring of Joy. And if you've already found that, then I hope this journey will help you remain connected for a lifetime and beyond. Because while it's very normal that we all reach our breaking point from time to time, one of the great miracles of living is this ability to experience renewal and transformation.

May we all be well as we journey forth into the great interconnected reality that we find ourselves in.

With Care,

Kristina Stone Kaiser

YOUR 90-DAY JOY JOURNEY!!

*A*s you begin your 90-Day Journey, this introduction will help you prepare and give you a sense of what to expect.

FORMAT

The Joy Journey offers 90 days of spiritual practices. Each day includes similar elements:

- Information about what materials you may want to bring to your practice
- A statement or phrase that sums up the day
- Information to help guide your practice
- A practice
- Reflection Prompts

Note:

- If you would like additional inspiration, Appendix B offers a series of songs, poetry books, and the like that have brought joy to this author.

- One thing that you'll often see is the mention of a "Joy Journal."

WHAT IS A JOY JOURNAL?

You are welcome to craft this part of the journey in a way that works for you. Many people find it helpful to have a special place designated for the things that are coming up during these 90 days. You might choose a:

- Physical journal
- Digital document on your computer
- Folder or binder with loose pieces of paper

And in fact, some people may prefer to skip the idea of a journal altogether. Choose a style that best supports you.

Whatever you decide, on occasion you'll be prompted to write or draw in your journal. When you see prompts like this, you are welcome to interpret these prompts using whatever format you've chosen. Or, another possibility still, you might decide to switch it up and use a different format that day. The gist of it is: Do what is going to work for you and embrace flexibility in your choice as needed.

WHAT IF I MISS A DAY?

Even as the commitment to this journey is just 10 minutes a day, you may have days where life gets away on you. Certainly, the recommendation is to be as consistent as possible since consistency is part of what moves something from a practice, to a habit, to a lifestyle. That said, if you miss a day, you have options:

1. Just keep going. If you missed Day 46, pick up again on Day 47.
2. Offer yourself 2 practices on one day in order to "make up" the practice.

3. Extend how long it takes to complete the 90-day journey. Maybe instead of ending on Day 90, you end on Day 91.

People have done all of these things depending on what worked best for them, and that is okay. All of this belongs.

WHAT IF I DON'T WANT TO DO SOME PARTICULAR PRACTICE?

The Joy Journey has been created with a lot of variety intentionally built in so that you can gain an increasingly reasonable idea about what works for you over the course of the 90 days. Some practices are going to be ones that really resonate with you. Others might leave you saying to yourself, "That was nice." And at other times you might simply say, "Meh."

Now interestingly, there is no real consensus about what is a highly resonating practice and what is just meh. The factors here are numerous—personality, season of life, how you're feeling at the time you do the practice, etc. If there was only one way to get to joy, we'd just offer that one thing and do it for 90 straight days!

So...if you come to a practice and you are skeptical about giving it a try, one possibility is to maybe just give it a try. It's not uncommon for people to say, "I wasn't sure if I would like that but wow! That really did something for me." Also, you'll see early on that options are offered. The door is always open for modifications to any practice.

That being said, if you hit one that you know you cannot do for any reason, consider repeating a practice from a previous day. This way you'll continue to build joy into your life as a lifestyle, and you'll continue to become adept at choosing what suits this moment now.

WHAT TIME OF DAY SHOULD I PRACTICE?

There is no right or wrong answer here unless the time you choose doesn't work for you. (That is the "wrong" time!) The key here is to decide on a time and then...protect that time. You are going to be tempted to schedule over it, to skip it, to skim it, or even just try to remember to keep the practice in mind for some later time in the day. But my suggestion to you is to give yourself the gift of these 10 minutes. And just to say it again, choosing a time that actually works for you really does matter. If you know that you are the sort of person that needs to start the day with spaciousness, then do that. If you have more time at lunch or at the end of the day, then maybe consider a later time in the day.

One logistical note if you choose a later time of day: You'll often see encouragement to keep thinking about some particular thing throughout the day. If you are engaging your practice later in the day, it's absolutely fine to allow that encouragement to apply to the following day.

IS THIS JOURNEY WRITTEN FOR ANY PARTICULAR GROUP OF PEOPLE?

This question could be asked a few other ways:

- Do I have to ascribe to some particular faith tradition?
- Should I be bothered that you don't use the same language as me?
- Can I be an atheist and still get something out of the experience?
- What if I identify as spiritually independent or interspiritual?
- Etc.

The Joy Journey was written for people from any religious, spiritual, or ethical tradition...or...from no tradition at all.

"How is this possible?!" you might ask.

Along the way, you will encounter moments where sacred texts are referenced from varying traditions. The texts are quoted as a means of offering us wisdom, and it is my hope that reading and engaging with these words will serve to enhance your experience and connection with your own belief system.

To help us along with this, you will see that I often use the words "The Divine" in an attempt to describe that which is beyond or more than us. "The Divine" is a stand-in for that which we call by many names or no name at all. Please feel welcome to bring the whole of yourself to what is written, allowing your own words and descriptions to enter in wherever you see reference to "the Divine."

One final word on this subject: My particular starting point includes the belief that we are all spiritual beings, whether we would refer to ourselves in this way or not. If this is a notion that does not resonate with you, please feel welcome to let that part of the reading go. It is my strong desire that everyone feel welcome on this Journey. I hope very much that you will feel at home, at peace, and at rest as you engage with this interspiritual reflection guide.

PRE-WORK

Celebration Worksheet (Appendix A). You'll soon become familiar with the rhythms built into the Journey, including a celebration day, which occurs every 7th day. We also make a big deal of coming to the end of 21 days (how long it takes to form a habit,) and at the end of 30, 60, and 90 days (the length of time it takes for something to become a lifestyle.) On some of those celebration days, you'll see an invitation to offer yourself an extra amount of intentional celebration.

The Celebration Worksheet is there to help you consider ahead of time what you really enjoy so that, if you aren't sure what you might do to celebrate, you can refer back to your list for inspiration.

Choosing a Joy Song/s. On occasion, the Spiritual Practice for the day will include interaction with music. You are invited to choose for yourself a song or two (or even an entire playlist) that will become your designated Joy Song/s. In considering what you might want to choose, ask yourself what song/s you know that instantly bring/s a smile to your face and cause you to want to move your body. And if you would find it useful, Appendix B offers a list of songs that have been sources of joy for this author.

ONE MORE POSSIBILITY: SCHEDULING YOUR FIRST ONE-ON-ONE

A one-on-one is a 60-minute session between you and a Spiritual Director. The word "director" is a bit of a misnomer, but a Spiritual Director is someone who has been trained to accompany another along their spiritual journey, to listen deeply and attentively, and to ask questions that will help you draw from the inner well within you.

Note: Spiritual Directors usually have an hourly fee based on their level of experience and the cost of living in their area; however, should you find that their fee is too much for you, many are willing to work on a sliding scale.

It is recommended that you add 3 one-on-one sessions to your 90-day Journey. Typically, these are scheduled as follows:

- About 2 weeks
- 8 weeks
- Between Day 87 and Day 90, or just a day or two after Day 90

The one-on-one sessions are invaluable for solidifying what is going on for you and making meaning of your experience, so I very much hope you will take this extra step.

To schedule a one-on-one, email info@tendingme.com or go to the Joy Journey page at https://www.tendingme.com/joy-journey.

TIME TO GET STARTED!

Okay, dear Joy Journeyer, hopefully you are feeling ready to begin. What you will find on the pages that follow has come about as a result of my own journey in pursuing joy amidst the struggles. It's a compilation of classes, videos, meditations, workshops, and retreats I've offered, all of it steeped in research that, I must confess, was some of the most fun I've ever had.

In the end, the Joy Journey became the subject of my doctoral project where I had the privilege of trying out these ideas with others. Overwhelmingly, participants reported up to a 40% increase in their overall joy in up to 6 areas of life. After completing that project, I couldn't help but notice the vast number of people who would begin sharing in casual conversation about how they weren't feeling themselves lately.

For a myriad of reasons, we all lose our connection to joy sometimes. May the next 90 days bring you back into relationship with yourself, with others, and with the Divine. May something open up for you over the course of this journey. May you find yourself back in touch with Joy, not merely as an intense emotional experience, but as an integral part of who you are.

WEEK 1

AWARENESS

DAY 1: DELIGHT IN YOUR LIFE

A GUIDED MEDITATION

What to bring to your practice: *A comfortable space*

Joy is one of the great gifts of life.

As we begin our journey, we begin with awareness. And as it turns out, there are many ways to be aware—our surroundings, our bodies, our thoughts, our feelings...

And so, here in this moment, begin to breathe deeply. When we breathe, so many good things occur in our bodies. On the inhalation, our heart rate increases—and so when we're feeling a bit sleepy, even just taking a few good breaths can help us get the energy flowing again.

From a spiritual perspective, faith traditions around the world recognize breath as a sort of life force. And so take some time now to inhale, taking breath down into the core of your being, filling every part of you with life.

And then exhale, allowing the toxins to leave your body. It's said that 70% of the toxins in our body are emitted through our exhales.

With every single breath we take, we inhale life and exhale toxicity. Over and over again.

In this moment, and the next, and now the next, we offer our attention—we offer our awareness—to the breath, and to the miracle of breath in our lives.

Let's take another moment to be aware of our breath. You may even wish to think to yourself: Breathing in. Breathing out. Or: Life in. Toxins out. Take a moment now…

…Having done that, I invite you now to gently begin to shift your awareness to the events of the last few hours. And as you consider this time that has passed, begin to ask yourself: What has been good?

Keep in mind—your response doesn't have to be fancy. It may be the warm glow of a nightlight, that first sip of coffee, or the feeling of warm water on your skin. Perhaps it was the sound of birds chirping, the pitter-patter of little feet, or the realization that today was a great day for wearing your favorite shirt.

Begin to let the experience of the day enter into your awareness. Ask yourself: what about my day has been good? I'll leave you another moment…

Now offer yourself another energizing inhale, breathing life in and letting toxins out.

…You have just done a very good thing. You've given yourself the gift of taking time to delight in your life.

As you go about the rest of your day, try to do this a few more times. Sometimes people find it helpful to try to pause somewhere along the lines of morning, noon, and night. But what this looks like in your life can vary. Most of us have a few natural pauses in our day that we offer ourselves in order to take care of our needs, whether we're hungry, thirsty, or just in need of a moment to sit still. When these natural pauses occur for you today, maybe take a moment to breathe life in, exhale toxins out, and ask yourself: What is good about my day?

Because in the end, joy is one of the great gifts of life.

DAY 2: THE TRUTH OF WHAT IS

What to bring to your practice: *Joy Journal*

Truth is the doorway to possibility.

O ur joy theme for this week is "Awareness." Yesterday we took some time to simply become aware of what was "good" in our lives, anything that was bringing joy, comfort, coziness, or peace.

Today we're going to allow our awareness to focus on the truth of what is, and we do this because naming our truth is an important part of awareness.

The trouble, however, is that most of us, believing we are helping ourselves, tend to deny our truths. We do this in order to repress experiences and feelings that we perceive as anything from inconvenient to outside of how we thought things were supposed to be. In spiritual circles, we sometimes refer to this as "spiritual bypassing" or "toxic positivity." Terms like these begin to cue us into the fact that denial does us no earthly—or spiritual—good.

What does do us good, however, is naming what truly is, for in doing so, we open the door to possibility.

PRACTICE

And so below you'll find a list of possible places where we might feel unaware of our truth from time to time. Using your Joy Journal, take some time to consider one or more of the Reflection Prompts below. And when you've named your truth, maybe take another moment to ask yourself: What is the significance of becoming aware of, and naming, this truth?

- *What am I feeling?*
- *What do I need?*
- *Do I feel angry or hurt in any way?*
- *What do I love?*
- *And again: What do I need?*
- *What is the significance of becoming aware of and naming these truths?*

If it would serve you, repeat this activity as many times today as you would like.

DAY 3: THE DIVINE IN ALL THINGS

What to bring to your practice: *Access to nature*
Optional: *Joy Journal, art supplies, camera, etc.*

We live in joy when we begin to see the Divine in all things.

oday we continue on our Joy Journey, allowing more of our lives to enter into our awareness.

One excellent way to put ourselves in touch with the gift of living is to turn our attention towards the great outdoors. Experiences in nature are an essential part of our well-being, and we're predisposed to want to connect with living things. We can imagine, then, that if we don't offer attention to this part of ourselves, our ability to feel as though we are living our lives to the full becomes stunted.

And so today, we use our senses to turn our attention outward.

PRACTICE

The invitation: Get outdoors. (If this isn't possible, opening a window or even sitting near a window will do.) If you'd like, bring along your Joy Journal and art supplies, finding yourself a nice sit spot. Or, consider taking a slow, mindful walk, noticing what's around you and possibly even taking a photo or two.

Whatever you choose, you may wish to return to the life-giving breaths of Day 1, allowing that life-energy to flow through you: Life in. Toxins out.

After a few of these breaths, take some time to look around. Ask yourself:

- *What do you see?*
- *How is the touch of the Divine present in what you see?*
- *What inspiration does this realization offer you?*

When we take time to become aware, we often find Divine Presence in a surprising number of places. Our sense of connection in the world grows, and as this happens, our joy increases.

Close your practice today with an offering of gratitude, whether that be a smile, a prayer, or even a tipping of your hat to the trees.

DAY 4: SUFFERING AND JOY

What to bring to your practice: *A comfortable space*

To live is to be in a constant state of transformation.

*W*ith living comes hope. Where our spiritual lives are concerned, we may hope that spiritual practices will help us avoid negative feelings. We may hope that our connection to these practices and to Source (the Divine) will take away the difficulties of life—or at least ease those difficulties significantly.

The Buddhist tradition tells us that suffering is inevitable. Pause here to notice what arises in you as you consider these words: Suffering is inevitable.

- What do you notice in your body?
- What do your thoughts tell you?
- Who or what comes to mind?

In the Christian tradition, Jesus tells us that:

...unless a kernel of wheat falls to the ground and dies, it remains only a single seed. But if it dies, it produces many seeds. —John 12:24 (NIV)

We might ask ourselves, then, "What does it mean for the death of something to become the birth of many somethings?"

Notably, the world around us offers numerous examples: Fallen leaves become nutrients for the soil. Decaying pine needles offer blueberry plants the acid they need to thrive. All around us there are examples of passing-away-things transforming in order to bring about new life.

And if this is true in the world around us, might this also be true in our own lives—that calms really do come after the storm, that joy really does come in the proverbial morning?

And if this is so, how do we journey ahead, not getting stuck in wanting things to remain as they were, but embracing this constant transformation of all things?

A couple of days ago, we practiced doing a little truth-telling, asking ourselves what truths may exist, even if we've been avoiding them.

Let's take a few moments to allow this idea of transformation to take deeper root in us. As we've been saying throughout this week, to inhale is to take life into the body and to exhale is to let toxins out.

And so, on your inhale, silently say the word: *Life*

And on the exhale, silently say the word: *Transformed*

If you'd like, feel free to close your eyes:

Inhale: *Life*

Exhale: *Transformed*

You can repeat this as many times as you'd like, returning to it throughout the day when you find yourself in particularly difficult moments.

DAY 5: MY PRESENT MOMENT

A GUIDED MEDITATION

What to bring to your practice: *A comfortable space*

Setting an intention for our day helps us to live intentional lives.

*T*his week, our exploration of joy involves the practice of awareness, and oftentimes, awareness involves our senses: What can we see, feel, hear, smell, taste...

Really taking in the world around us is invigorating. Catching the sound of birds as you stumble out of bed is joyful, much more joyful than bemoaning the fact that another morning has come. Looking up from our phones and seeing a bright moon shining through our window, taking in the smell of the air as we step outside, savoring that first bite of food, snuggling into a cozy blanket...when we engage our senses, the opportunity for life to become delightful increases. And the more we invest ourselves in this practice, the more that this becomes our experience of life.

And, thankfully for us, we don't have to wait for the rest of our lives to happen. We can begin right now—and then we can begin again a bit later today, and again, a bit after that, over and over again, for the rest of our lives.

And so let's take a moment now. Inhale life deep into the core of your body, exhale the toxins that have been building up since your last good exhale, and as you do, open your awareness to your senses. What is absolutely delightful about this moment now? Is it the feel of your chair or your clothes? Is it a sound you can hear? Is it something you can see? Is it something you can taste or something you can smell? What is delightful about this moment now?

…You may notice that whatever came to mind just now was possibly quite ordinary, which is absolutely okay. Not every moment of our lives is going to be a symphony playing to the backdrop of an elaborate fireworks display. Much of our lives are filled with simple joys. The question is, how many of them will we take the time to enjoy?

This is a practice you can return to again and again, allowing your senses to open your awareness to divine joy, or, if you prefer, Divine Joy.

DAY 6: THE BODY'S STORY

What to bring to your practice: *Joy Song, a comfortable space*

Allow your dancing to free you.

Our level of comfort with dancing is often tied to our cultures, families of origins, and spiritual communities. Some of us may have even taken a vow not to dance. (If this is you, I invite you to translate today's practice in a way that's right for you—maybe offering yourself a flow meditation or taking an intentional walk where each step is about naming the bondages you've become aware of today and stepping out of your chains as you walk.)

If dance is possible, however, the type of movement we're talking about is about naming our traumas, telling our stories, and allowing that truth-telling to offer us something internally. Our external action becomes representative of an internal action.

PRACTICE

And so first:

- Take a moment to pause and practice a little truth-telling right now, beginning first by centering and grounding yourself with the breath: Life in. Toxins out.

And when you are ready:

- What is something that feels heavy, painful, or troubling to you right now?

Once you have named your truth, allow yourself to incorporate movement using the Joy Song you chose as part of your Pre-Work from the Introduction. It may well be that you feel yourself wanting to stomp on the trauma, to shake it off, or something else. Perhaps your movement gives way to not moving at all. Whatever happens, allow yourself to notice how your body wants—and even chooses—to move.

- *As your time of movement comes to a close, take a moment to consider what this time has meant to you.*

And if you wish, return to this practice whenever you like, allowing your dancing to free you.

DAY 7: CELEBRATING AND SAVORING

What to bring to your practice: *Joy Journal*

Choose awareness. Choose joy.

oday we celebrate! You've walked through an entire week of deepening and strengthening your awareness muscle. You've taken time to breathe, to name your truths, to engage your senses, and to move your body, allowing your external world to mirror your internal world and spiritual self. These are important practices that you'll be able to use again and again on your Joy Journey.

But for today, we pause to celebrate this experience of making the choice to become aware, of choosing to live in joy.

As we do that, our practice for today invites us to name the ways in which others have spoken good into our lives. Psychologists tell us that our brains tend to more readily remember that which has been negative in our lives. We're told that if we don't spend at least 15 seconds savoring the good things that happen to us, that we will lose them. This means that, while we may often consider our lives to be a mixed bag, in the end, we'll tend to assume that the bag is weighted towards the negative. But not today!

Today, we take a moment to bring the good back into our awareness by way of calling to mind at least five things that others have complimented us on. We're going to take some time to celebrate, savor and enjoy the ways in which we are loved and appreciated by others.

PRACTICE

- *What are 5 things that others have complimented you on?*
- *When your list is complete, take a bit of time to savor what has come to mind, to enjoy it and love that aspect of who you are.*

Happy Celebrating!

WEEK 2

MINDFULNESS

DAY 8: THE PRACTICE OF LETTING GO

A GUIDED MEDITATION

What to bring to your practice: *A comfortable space*

Notice your thoughts so that they don't carry you away.

$\mathcal{E}$quanimity is a word we sometimes use for this act of "not getting carried away." Others may call it "being nonjudgmental." Whatever words we use, the idea behind all of them is the same: Not every emotion or thought is worth reacting to.

But, as is often the case, the act of *not reacting to every little thing* is sometimes easier said than done.

- We see the look on someone's face and imagine it's about us.
- We play scenarios in our heads over and over again *as if* they were true.
- We ruminate.

The mind becomes a treadmill set to warp speed with no relief in sight.

Have you ever been on a treadmill set to the highest speed? If you have, then you may have noticed how difficult it becomes to keep up! Even when you're ready to stop, the treadmill doesn't have the ability to slow down on its own. If we, the operator, do not choose to hit the necessary buttons, nothing changes.

This week, we are going to do just that. We're going to slow down the treadmill. And in doing so, we're going to continue our journey towards increasing joy in everyday life.

And so, to begin, take a moment to arrive in this present moment by returning your attention to the breath. Our breath is a useful life force that wells up from within, always with us, always present. Take a moment to feel this life force, noticing the coolness of that breath as it enters your nostrils, making itself known on the back of the throat, and continuing down into the body, to the very center of your being.

And then, having taken that breath in, notice the short pause that naturally occurs between the inhale and the exhale, a moment where the body relishes this breath that's just been taken. As slight as this pause is, it reminds us of how natural it is for our bodies to pause, how it's built into the very essence of our being.

And yet, at the very same time, we are not meant to stay in this suspended state. Begin to notice now how your body naturally moves to exhale, effortlessly and easily letting go of the breath, just as readily as we had allowed the breath to enter our bodies.

In the same way that we first welcomed the inhale, we now welcome the exhale, not only allowing the breath to leave us, but also allowing tensions to leave our body as well. Each exhale offers us the opportunity to embrace the practice of letting go—whether we are letting go of thoughts, muscle tensions, demands, or something else. Take a few of these breaths, leaning into this practice of release on the exhale…

…And now, having taken some time to ground yourself using the breath, to further consider this practice of letting go, allow your attention to turn towards something that's been bothering you lately

—a thought, a person, or a struggle that's been keeping your mental treadmill active.

As that thing comes to mind, offer yourself the image of a leaf floating down the river. Imagine that leaf moving ever so slowly across the top of the water, effortlessly and easily flowing…

…With that lovely leaf in your mind's eye, hold gently this difficult thing that has kept your mental treadmill going lately, and allow it to become small enough to fit on this floating leaf. See it resting on the leaf, which has now begun to float down the river.

As you continue breathing, watch the leaf moving farther and farther away from you, moving along with the current of the water, becoming smaller and smaller to the naked eye as it drifts farther and farther away…until finally, it disappears from sight, until all you can see is a beautifully flowing river, until all that remains is this moment now…

…The river is peaceful. And hopefully, so is the mind. Now…does this mean that your problems no longer exist? Maybe. It's possible that this thing that's been bothering you doesn't need to return. But even if you will need to attend to this thing again, the good news is that it doesn't have to be something that carries *you* away.

The practice of mindfulness helps us increase our ability to coexist with our struggles, to experience both the goodness and the difficulties. Mindfulness allows us to hold it all in equanimity, to live in the middle of what actually is without being carried away by it. It opens the door for joy—for delight in living.

Though our mindfulness practice for today is coming to a close, feel welcome to stay in this space for as long as you wish, and to return to it as many times as you'd like.

DAY 9: LOOKING WITH CURIOSITY

What to bring to your practice: *Joy Journal*

What was, is no longer.
What is today, will not always be.
Take heart in the constant changing of things.

Faith traditions across the globe encourage us to look at the world through new eyes. In the Buddhist and Hindu traditions, this practice is called "Beginner's Mind," and it's what allows us to approach our lives with curiosity instead of rigidity.

…Speaking of rigidity…take a moment now to allow your breath to center you, taking in that sacred breath and then exhaling, letting go of rigidities and tensions in the body.

Now from this place, consider how easy it is to say of ourselves, "This is just the way I am. I've always been this way, and I'll never change." We find it equally easy to use this logic with others saying, "This is just the way *they* are; and they will never change."

But what if things aren't even exactly as they were yesterday? What if we, and everyone around us, have been just a little bit changed between yesterday and today?

Scientifically, we know this to be true. We know that our cells regenerate, some more frequently than others, but by the time 7 years has passed, each cell in our body has been made new at least once. And so, can we allow ourselves to become curious about this process of being made new? Can we develop the ability to wonder about it? How is our mind being made new? What is it that this present moment is offering us?

PRACTICE

Today I want to invite you to spend some time with your Joy Journals, offering yourself at least five tangible ways that you are not the same as you used to be. Maybe you used to despise tomatoes but now love them. Maybe you used to be a night owl and now are in bed before your friends. Consider what ideas you've had about yourself that may not be true anymore, allowing these things to come to mind without judgment. They are neither good nor bad. They just are. When you have completed your list, ask yourself:

- *What curiosities do these realizations bring up?*

Allow yourself to enjoy both your curiosities and your present self.

DAY 10: JOY THROUGH SAVORING

What to bring to your practice: *Access to nature, camera optional*

Paying attention brings appreciation, brings joy.

*J*oy is the unlimited essence of our being. For this reason, though we may sometimes speak of joy as "delight in living," there is both the possibility for Joy to make us a little bit happier and for Joy to be like a wellspring, as if coming from the very core of all things.

The word "Namaste" can be translated as *"the divine in me sees the divine in you."* One way we do this is by cultivating the ability to wonder about one another, to assume that we are all connected some- how, and to live into a more relational way of being.

The question is, can we embrace this notion of finding Joy by way of paying attention? And can we do that by engaging in the practice of savoring, by saying, "Ah yes, a lovely breeze, a singing bird, a kind person who opened the door for me…"

And then…can we choose to *really* savor it.

PRACTICE

Connecting with nature can also be a powerful way to both engage our appreciation and also deepen our awareness of Joy. It's what happens when we look up and out and all around.

- *What do we see?*
- *What do we notice that we otherwise would have missed?*

Is it some sort of reflection or shadow that's hitting uniquely in this moment now? Is it a movement? An insect? What is in your nearby, natural environment that is capturing your attention right now…now that you're paying attention to it?

- *If you have the ability, maybe take a picture or a video of this thing.*

Allow it to be something you return to, not only later today, but any other day you want. Let it remind you of the feeling you had when you discovered this natural beauty, how amazing it was to just become aware of its existence. Allow today to be a day that you ask yourself: What miracle is available to me, now that I'm paying attention?

DAY 11: COMPANIONING WHAT'S DIFFICULT

What to bring to your practice: *Joy Journal*

Being aware of what's troubling is a part of the journey.

John 16:33 in the Christian Bible quotes Jesus as saying, *"In this world you will have trouble."*

That is both a healthy dose of reality and also a hard pill to swallow, isn't it? Even as we can see that sorrow, trouble, and struggle are all around us, many of us continue to swim upstream, trying to force things to be "right," both for ourselves and for others. We don't want to be sad, and we don't want others to be sad.

But the truth of the matter is, to fight against the negative emotions we feel tends to do us more harm than good. We're far better off "riding the wave" of our emotions, allowing them to peak as we feel them to the full and then wane again as our circumstances change.

What we also know is that unacknowledged emotions tend to become little bits of triggerable trauma that live in the recesses of our hearts, minds, and bodies.

And so, though it may seem confusing and even counterintuitive, can we choose to become aware of—and name—our sorrows as an actual part of our Joy Journey? Or, might we at least accept that sometimes we have sorrows? Might we learn to name our emotions—to actually be able to say, "I'm feeling sad, angry, grieved, frustrated, ignored, taken advantage of…" And then, rather than trying to push those emotions back down or distract ourselves, what if we were able to sit with them for a moment, just to see what emerges?

PRACTICE

Let's give it a try right now. Once again, your practice begins by arriving fully here in this present moment. Breathe in that life-giving breath, exhale out the toxins, tensions in the body, and busyness of the mind. As you breathe, take note of whatever good actually exists here in this present moment.

Once you feel centered and grounded, take another moment to ask yourself, "Is it safe for me to acknowledge any negative emotions I have either been feeling or actively holding back?" If now is not a good time to ask this question, that's okay. You can always come back at another time when it does feel safe. But if you do feel your current moment will allow it, use the reflection prompt below to begin your practice:

- *"I feel — because —. This is a part of me. This is a part of my experience of life. The hard is all mixed up with the good."*

Continue speaking kindly, gently, and compassionately to yourself:

"This is acceptance. I am setting an intention to accept that this is a part of my experience. I don't have to ruminate about it. I don't have to roll the

story around in my head until I've completely exhausted myself. But I can name it. I can acknowledge it."

Earlier this week, we took some time to imagine one of our struggles floating down the river on a leaf. This is one of many ways of letting go.

In this moment now, we embrace a slightly different practice. Ask yourself:

- *Is there anything I need in order to help me move through this emotion?*

- *What will help me choose joy—not a false sense of happiness—but the ability to live in cooperation and equanimity with what really is?*

And then, when you are ready, one final reflection:

- *What will help me let go of what doesn't need to be here?*

Today's practice invites us to accept the truth while also letting go of anything we might be adding to it. Allow your inner wisdom to guide you...because this, too, belongs.

DAY 12: THE DELICIOUS GIFT OF LIFE

What to bring to your practice:
A food item or some other observable object

*May Joy come to the surface as we delight in the
deliciousness, the beauty, and the aroma of being alive*

*L*ife is a gift! This is something we know intuitively from a
very young age. The question is, how do we allow our daily
lives to reflect this reality? How do we take in the deliciousness of the day?

PRACTICE

Today's spiritual practice is a *meditation of the senses,* and it may well
turn out to be quite delicious!

To begin, first *pick a focus for your meditation*. In this case, I'll be continuing as if that focus is a food item.

Whatever you have chosen, allow yourself to begin to fully interact with your focus.

- *Take it in—look at its beauty.*
- *What is its color?*
- *What shape has it taken?*
- *What texture exists that you can observe?*
- *What makes it amazingly unique?*
- *Does it have a smell?* As you take in a good inhale, is there any aroma that meets and delights your nostrils?
- Beginning to eat now, try not to go too quickly. Really *taste* it. If the texture is enjoyable, enjoy it fully. Make noises, even, if you want! Ooh and ahh if the moment calls for it. This is your moment of indulgent enjoyment.
- …And when you have swallowed, *what remains?* Is there a taste that lingers? Perhaps a desire to get that next bite!

Many times a day, we rush through experiences that could be so much more enjoyable. But even washing the dishes can bring a certain enjoyment if we allow ourselves to relish the feel of the warm water on our skin or the birds chasing each other outside the window…or both!

Offer yourself these simple delights as many times a day as you can remember to do so.

DAY 13: MINDFUL WALKING

What to bring to your practice: *Space to walk, Joy Journal optional*

Goodness is all around.

Today, we continue our mindfulness theme by offering ourselves the spiritual practice of Mindful Walking. Certainly there are many ways to do this. You could:

- Pay attention to the *surface beneath you*
- Offer *attention to your body* as you walk—the feet, the calves, the upper legs, and so on
- Use a *centering phrase*, such as the one above
- *Practice appreciation* for the things you see around you
- *Observe your emotions or thoughts*

In seeing a list like this, perhaps you may feel tempted to try all of them at once. The good news is, you can return to mindful walking anytime you'd like. So try one, and then try something else on a different day.

You may also ask yourself, "Am I supposed to go outside for this?" And the good news is, there's no right or wrong answer. Mindfulness walks can occur anywhere. So do what works best for you.

But when we take the time to move mindfully, it's remarkable how quickly we may find our mood and stress levels lifting. Our brains so easily find themselves on autopilot and even distracted. With this practice, we can bring ourselves back to this moment now while also discovering the goodness that exists all around us.

PRACTICE

- *Offer yourself 5 to 10 minutes of mindful walking.*
- *And then, if you'd like, take some time to journal about your experience.*

DAY 14: MUSICAL MINDFULNESS

What to bring to your practice: *Joy Song*

Music has the power to revitalize us from the inside out.

*I*t's time to celebrate! We've been on our Joy Journey for 14 days now, which has included 6 days of mindfulness practices. Congratulations! Imagine confetti (*that you don't have to clean up*) here.

PRACTICE

Today's spiritual practice involves offering yourself some musical engagement.

- *Begin by cueing up your Joy Song.*

- As you listen, allow yourself to *become a part of the experience, hearing* the words, *feeling* the music in your body.
- If you feel an urge to move your body or respond in any way, give yourself *permission to follow that urge.*

Take the song in as many times as you'd like, noticing what happens in your mind, body, and heart as you interact. Allow the music to revitalize you from the inside out.

WEEK 3

GRATITUDE

DAY 15: GRATITUDE

A GUIDED MEDITATION

What to bring to your practice: *A comfortable space*

Joy is what happens when we are able to hold both the difficult and the good.

*W*elcome to the third week of our Joy Journey! Our theme for this week is gratitude.

Gratitude, it turns out, is an essential part of a life where Joy can actually be the unlimited essence of our being. It helps us relish our experiences, connect with the people around us, appreciate the goodness that exists in our lives, and on and on. Gratitude can be defined as appreciation under any circumstance. And if all of this isn't reason enough to develop a practice of gratitude, here's one more: Practicing gratitude before bed can even help you sleep better!

Today, we'll engage this practice of gratitude through the lens of meditation. So from wherever you are, begin to settle into your space, allowing yourself to rest in a comfortable position so that your body can rest into a posture of receiving. For you, this may mean open hands, an uplifted heart, or even just a simple smile in the corners of the mouth or eyes.

Allow yourself to feel the support of whatever is beneath you, and when you are ready, begin to turn your attention towards gratefulness for this secure base of support that is beneath you. In savoring this feeling of gratitude, inhale deeply, allowing that life-giving breath to fill you. This life force is yet another little thing to be grateful for. And so, even here, we pause briefly in gratitude...

...Again we bring that energizing breath into the body, and then exhale our stresses, our toxins, and our tensions. What a gift and a miracle it is that our bodies do this so automatically. Without any attention at all, our bodies breathe, taking in that which we need to thrive and letting out that which would otherwise poison our bodies.

And that is only one part of how our bodies function so automatically. Consider the miracle that is your body—all of the various systems that keep you going—the cardiovascular system, the digestive system, the respiratory system, the nervous system...so many parts working together to form the collective whole that is you...We pause here to rest in gratitude for how our bodies do so much more for us than we're often aware of...

...Let us also turn our attention to the miracle of the abundance that exists around us. As we do this, we remember again that our gratefulness does not ignore or deny the negative aspects of life. It doesn't mean that we shouldn't have aspirations, hopes, and dreams. All of these needs and desires remain and fit into the matrix of our lives. We just don't want to exclude that which *is* abundant in our lives.

And so, the clothes that protect us in such a variety of circumstances, the toothbrush that offers its service, no matter what we've eaten that day or how bad our breath may be. The products we use as we shower and prepare for the day. In fact—how many lives have touched ours between our waking and our breakfast? Is it 50? 100? How many hands were instrumental in bringing us our coffee, milk, tea, or juice? How many lives, human, animal, and plant alike, are now connected to ours?

In considering this broader picture, we pause here to be grateful for this wide network of beings, realizing how we all play together, even when we've paid it no mind whatsoever. It all just works together, doing what it does naturally.

This great web of connection, all held together by an invisible nucleus, might be called by many names. Today we'll call it Joy—the unlimited essence of our being—the well of Life from which we all spring and have our being. How grand it is!

And so we pause to be grateful for these many gifts, all working together, creating goodness both within us as well as far beyond us. Take a moment or two to relish in whatever is rising up within you personally…

As we conclude our practice today, we offer a bow of the head, acknowledging all of this goodness that exists around us, extending our gratitude for these many gifts.

DAY 16: GRATITUDE LISTS

What to bring to your practice: *Joy Journal*

Find what brings a smile to your face
and then live deeply into the enjoyment of your discovery.

*J*oy can be defined both as "the unlimited essence of our being" and also as "the experience of a positive emotion that manifests through physical expressions such as smiling, laughing, and energetic movement."

Throughout these 90 Days, our aim is to experience an increase of joy in both of these ways—both as a primary source of Life as well as an emotion that spontaneously wells up as we feel delight.

But, of course, life is complex! At times, we may be more aware of our spiritual selves than our physical selves. At other times, it may be just the opposite. And yet somehow, regardless of our levels of awareness in any given moment, all of it is wonderfully intertwined and connected.

PRACTICE

- *Gratitude List of 20 Things*

Moments of pause and reflection can be powerful ways to allow our physical and spiritual worlds to more profoundly come into our awareness. And so, in continuing to explore this theme of gratitude, today we're going to offer ourselves the practice of a gratitude list, naming 20 things that we're grateful for. **Note:** Try not to think about it too hard—just twenty things off the top of your head that you're grateful for.

To begin, once again, allow yourself a bit of space, slowing down from the pace of life, pausing from the work of the day, and allowing yourself to exhale right into the heart of this moment now. You are here. This time is not full or busy in any way. It's just you and Presence. When you are ready, you can begin your gratitude list.

When your list is complete, rather than moving on too quickly, allow yourself another moment or two to *really savor and enjoy these amazing things that you have named for yourself.*

For the day (and beyond):

- *Allow your list to act as an anchor for you in those moments where joy feels harder to find.*

DAY 17: THE GIFT OF LIVING

What to bring to your practice: *Joy Journal*

JOY COMES TO VISIT
Flowers burst and bloom
Bright and divine in color
Joy comes to visit

Trees dance on breezes
Cool and invigorated,
Wonder arises
—August 2022

*D*o you ever have one of those days where you feel as though everything rests on your shoulders? We have a lot of sayings in our world that support this idea:

- It's all up to you now, kid.
- Don't forget, we're all counting on you.
- If it's gonna be anyone, it's gotta be you.

From a young age, we're challenged with the task of measuring up. And that constant pursuit to be "at the top of our field" is a lot of pressure, a pressure that often causes us to have a hyper-developed relationship with our critical voice.

So let's just put that down for a moment. If you need to pick it up again later on, you can. But in this moment now, can you allow there to be nothing else between you and Joy—the unlimited essence of your being. As you lighten your load, once again begin to savor your inhale and exhale, that miraculous life flowing in and out of you.

Isn't it grand? You're alive! You're here!

In addition to savoring that gift of life, leave yourself space to also welcome whatever else is true in this moment. We want to continue to develop that practice of including the whole of our lives, remembering that joy is what happens when we hold both the difficult and the good.

PRACTICE

With one more deep and glorious inhale, once again read the poem, *"Joy Comes to Visit"* from above. As you do, pause to notice:

- *What word or phrase stands out to you right now?*

Read the poem again. This time, ask yourself:

- *"Why is this word or phrase standing out to you?"*

Read the poem yet a 3rd time.

- *Is there anything you're feeling inspired to do or not do as you, once again, consider the poem?*

Reading the poem just one last time, savoring the presence of Spirit in your life:

- *What do you want to take with you as you move into the rest of your day?*

DAY 18: THIS IS DIFFICULT

What to bring to your practice: *A comfortable space*

When difficulties happen, compassion carries us through.

In the movie *Innocent Voices (2004)*, we're given a window into what it was like to live in El Salvador during the Civil War of the 1980's. We quickly begin to see how the events of a day can take a dramatic turn, from children running and laughing through fields to children lying on hot metal rooftops, from families eating dinner together and chatting happily, to those very same families hiding behind mattresses as bullets riddle their homes. These are extreme examples of "bad things," and though hard to watch, they show us the poignant reality that the "good" and "bad" of our lives are intermingled together. Each of us holds the capacity for laughter and tears at the exact same time, which can be a bit confusing!

In trying to help us cultivate a personal container that can hold all of this complexity at once, sometimes we are offered the opportunity to view our emotions, not as "good" or "bad," but as neutral.

The same can be said for our experiences. There may be some outcomes that we ultimately perceive as "good." But there may also be outcomes, even from that very same situation, that we will ultimately perceive as "bad." It's complex.

A "bad" situation might bring us closer together with someone we care about. A "good" job promotion might cause us to have to spend more time away from home. What is "good?" What is "bad?" What are the criteria for these labels?

PRACTICE

Today's spiritual practice: *This is difficult.*

For today, rather than trying to figure anything out, if only for a moment, we're simply going to rest in the embrace of Compassion, of Loving Kindness. We're setting an intention to rest in the arms of not-being-alone.

As you begin to breathe slowly, once again remember: There is a wellspring of Joy that resides within us. It is the unlimited essence of your being. And so, in taking a moment to name any emotion within you that might be causing you pain, rather than shying away from it, repressing it, locking it away for a later time—instead of any (or all) of that—put a hand over your heart.

Connect with the inner wellspring of your being. You are not alone. Faith, Joy, Love—the One that you call by many names, one name, or no name at all—is with you. There is space for all of you here in this moment—for all of you and all of your stories, for all of you and each of your emotions.

To be joyful does not mean that you must deny some other part of you. Rather, the whole of you can support the all of you. And so, allowing that breath to remind you of this incredible Life Source within, with your hand over your heart, and with Love and Compassion as your companion, allow yourself to say, *"This is difficult"*—to simply be held, to not be alone. Allow even yourself to be with yourself.

Do this as many times as you need to, both now and in the future. Allow yourself to be held in those moments that feel overwhelming and difficult.

- *As you engage this practice, notice how your whole self responds.*
- *What do you notice physically? Emotionally? Mentally? Spiritually?*

DAY 19: A FEAST OF THE SENSES

What to bring to your practice: *Your surroundings*

You're alive. Enjoy it!

*E*arlier this week we noted that joy is what happens when we're able to hold both the difficult and the good, and then, we took some time to be grateful for our lives.

This is an important point.

Gratitude is not about suppressing the negative in our lives. It's about making the choice to offer our awareness to both the positive and the negative. And in fact, yesterday's spiritual practice was all about not ignoring or denying what is difficult in our lives.

Having begun to practice including—and living with—the difficult, today we turn our attention towards taking time to appreciate the positive. We take on the practice of setting an intention to enjoy our lives.

In the book of Ecclesiastes, in the Hebrew Bible (also known as the Old Testament of the Christian Bible) in a section called Writings, or Ketuvim, we hear this from King Solomon on the topic of enjoyment:

> So I commend the enjoyment of life, because there is nothing better for a person under the sun than to eat and drink and be glad. Then joy will accompany them in their toil all the days of the life God has given them under the sun. —Ecclesiastes 8:15 (NIV)

And so, today, our spiritual practice is to enjoy life by offering ourselves a feast of the senses!

And the amazing thing about feasting is that it can be done in many ways. In the most literal sense, we can feast on food. We can also feast our eyes, our ears, or any other part of us that can sense and enjoy. All we have to do is pick an object to focus our attention on. That could be a symphony, the sound of flowing water, the way the light shines so as to cast a shadow or a reflection. It could also be something delicious, or the luxurious feel of something soft and cushy. It could be something spectacular, or incredibly ordinary. And if there's absolutely nothing in our present moment that we could feast upon, perhaps there is the memory of something that can offer us a Divine Feast.

Whatever you choose, the idea is to allow yourself to be fully present to that focus and to "have your fill" of it, to savor it, to experience a particular *joie de vivre*—a delight in living.

PRACTICE

Consider what your *feast of the senses* will be today. What exists around you that you can enjoy, even relish in, allowing your senses to spark and ignite the Joy within?

Once you have picked your feasting subject, go ahead and *"dig in."* Enjoy it for the sake of enjoyment and nothing more. *Revel* in that enjoyment. *Be fully present* to it, fully taking in this moment now. You'll know you are done when you feel the fullness of satisfaction.

Take care not to end before the moment is complete, and then eventually close your practice with one deep and fulfilling sacred breath.

- *When your practice is complete, pause to notice how this experience has affected you. What do you notice physically? Emotionally? Mentally? Spiritually?*

As usual, return to this experience of feasting frequently. Because after all, as long as you're alive, you might as well enjoy it.

DAY 20: LIFE ABUNDANT

What to bring to your practice: *A wall, a chair, or another person to support you*

Gratitude is a path that leads to wider paths.

*E*ach of us knows all too well the mind's capacity for critical thinking, because the ability to (skillfully) focus on fault and lack has become an object of praise in our society. And this ability within us certainly has its uses, protecting us and helping us to navigate the waters of life. Three cheers for the analytical mind!

But balance is such an important part of life, isn't it? It turns out that the opposite of lack is abundance. And in life, our aim is to strike a balance between these things—an ability to see each of them equally, which means we have to exercise our ability to see abundance.

PRACTICE

Today's spiritual practice involves allowing the use of your body to become a metaphor for all of life. Choose one of the poses below:

Tree pose.

- *Tree pose*

Or if you prefer to keep both feet on the ground:

- *Mountain pose*

Note: Please read the entire lesson for the day before beginning your practice.

Choose one or both of these positions to anchor your practice today, allowing yourself to embody the qualities of the pose(s).

You are stable, whether it's your roots that connect you solidly to the ground of your being, or the base of your mountain that is supporting your sense of stability. While holding your position(s) of choice, enjoy a few life-giving inhales and critical-releasing exhales. This is your moment to rest from analyzing and to embrace abundance.

Mountain pose.

Note: If you are in tree pose, the possibility exists that you may fall out of balance during your practice. If this happens, you have an abundance of choices. You might choose to return to tree pose, to switch to mountain pose, to use a wall or a chair for support, or even to enlist the help of another person. Even in losing our balance there is abundance. This, too, belongs.

From this rooted and grounded space:

- *What abundances can you name in your life?*

Allow the possibilities to flow as you engage in this position of balance. Begin to see the broader picture. You are breathing. Is there any abundance there? What gifts are present for you today? What are you feeling particularly grateful for?

When your time of noticing and naming your abundances is complete, offer yourself one more Joy-connecting breath and close your practice, remembering that you can return to this place any time you feel the need for a little perspective.

DAY 21: CELEBRATING THE LITTLE THINGS

What to bring to your practice: *Your voice*

Your life is precious and worth living.

 elcome to the end of the 3rd Week of your Joy Journey! Twenty-one days of tending to the very essence of your being! They say it takes 21 days to make something a habit and 90 days to turn something into a lifestyle, which means you are well on your way to living into your *joie de vivre*.

As we see noted above, life is precious. Intrinsically, we know this. But of course, we don't only want to *know* it. We want to live it out. Is today chock full of meetings? Are there people fighting all around you? Do you feel ill? These are the sorts of things we may feel tempted to just try and get through. But then how many days will we have lost to just surviving? This is where gratitude, in even the little things, can be helpful.

Today's spiritual practice is called *"The Living Ah,"* which is so simple to do and brings such joy! All you do is take in one of those life-giving breaths, just as we've been doing the last several weeks, and then, on the exhale, allow yourself to say out loud, "Ahhhhhhh…." And you can make that "Ah" as long or as short as you'd like. There are no right or wrong ways to do it. Your "Ah" could be high, low, moving high to low or low to high. It could mimic the sound of a sigh. However you would like to "Ah" is completely up to you.

And the lovely thing about *"The Living Ah"* is that it fits so well into the pauses of our days, allowing us to release our tensions in both an internal and an external way.

PRACTICE

And so, to begin, offer yourself two or three of these *Living Ah's* now, inhaling, and then audibly allowing your "Ah…" to carry on your exhale.

Having done that, as you settle for a moment, if there are any *gratitudes or any causes for celebration,* allow them to come to mind, offering them as a part of your practice today.

When you are ready, close with *one or two more Living Ah's,* allowing yourself to embrace the preciousness of the day and the life you are living.

WEEK 4

REFRAMING & PERSPECTIVE

DAY 22: YOU CAN

A GUIDED MEDITATION

What to bring to your practice: *A comfortable space*

Our perception affects our seeing.

*W*elcome to the 4th week of your journey to discovering a deeper connection to Joy—to the very essence of your being, to the daily delights that each day brings.

This week we will be taking time to hone in on the idea of reframing, which allows us to look again, with a beginner's mind, with child-like wonder, with the understanding that there may well be more we have yet to see, to know, to learn, to feel…

And so as we begin, take a moment to celebrate: You are alive!

And rather than rushing past this beautiful truth, really enjoy it. Breathe it in, literally taking life into your body, allowing the breath to reach all the way down to the tips of your fingers and toes. And then as you exhale, exhale with great joy, allowing the weights you are carrying to be put down for a bit.

And once you have taken in a couple of these wonderfully grounding breaths, begin to breathe naturally again.

Today we are going to be sitting with the phrase: *You Can.*

Many of us know all too well the feeling of being limited. We understand it well because each of us lives in a world where our small-self experiences limits. Limits on our time, our money, our energy. We understand the concept of limited resources.

But our small self is not the only story. There is also our Spirit self. And the Spirit within is limitless—beyond time, beyond the understandings of this world.

Together then, what we find is that the "small self" and the "Spirit self" create paradox. We are both limited and limitless all at the same time. And so, though it is often tempting for us to focus on what "we can't" in our lives, today we shift our perspective to consider what "we can," because, in truth, the way we see the world is also the way we experience the world. Our perception affects our seeing.

And so to begin: You can acknowledge.
You can acknowledge your full range of emotions.
You can acknowledge both your disappointments and your triumphs.
You can acknowledge your desires and your contentedness.
Take a moment to notice what would like to be acknowledged
right now.

Not only can you acknowledge, you can know.
You can know the moments that changed your life.
You can know that you are changing another's life.
You can know the facts of the past and the predictions of the future.
As we pause here together, what do you know right now?

~

You can acknowledge. You can know. And you can also become.
You can evolve and change.
You can experience life made new.
You can learn and grow, day after day and season after season.
In what ways have you experienced transformation recently?

~

With heart wide open, as if pointed towards the sun, you can be free.
You can be forgiven. And you can forgive.
You can see, with spiritual eyes, the light of all that is around you.
You can hear with compassionate ears the story that needs to be told.
You can marvel at the continual change that is going on in everyone
and everything.
And in all of it, you can let go. Take some time to let go now.

~

You who are filled with light and love, you can make a difference.
You can improve the world, one act of goodness at a time.
You can encourage the life of another.
You can tend to the things that are before you.
You can pause. And in the pause, you can be empowered.
Let us be empowered together.

~

Thank you for your practice today. May your days be filled with new
ways to see and experience the world around you.

DAY 23: STORIES WE TELL OURSELVES

What to bring to your practice: *Joy Journal*

The negative story is not my only story.

oday we continue our Joy Journey by examining the stories we tell ourselves, looking to see if there is anything we might want to get a bit more perspective on.

A few notes about "the stories we tell ourselves":

It may be that you've heard this called by other names:

- Necessary suffering and unnecessary suffering
- Clean pain and dirty pain
- Thought distortions and affirmations

All of this language is getting at the same thing. We tend to tell ourselves a story and then play that story over and over again in our heads:

- It's not going to work out.
- Things aren't going to go well.
- I'm never going to get it done, etc.

And, of course, we have reasons for why we let these scripts play out in our head. But today we are going to include that which may be more difficult for us to rehearse in our heads, because when we tell ourselves these more positive stories, we actually get more done. We're more focused. We feel better about ourselves. Our anxiety levels decrease. So many benefits!

PRACTICE

And so to begin, as we often do, offer yourself a moment of centering. Breathe deeply, opening your senses. What can you hear? What can you feel? What can you see? When you feel ready, take some time with the reflection prompts below:

- *What is the story I'm telling myself?*
- *Are there any alternative stories to the one I've been telling myself?*
- *Is there a more helpful story for me to tell myself?*

DAY 24: FINDING JOY EVERYWHERE

What to bring to your practice: *A nature-connected space, Joy Journal*

STIR UP YOUR JOY
All who are weary
Take a walk in the garden
Be warmed by the fire

Listen to the birds
Let the breeze stir up your joy
Leap with the crickets

Your smile will return
Laughter will rise up in you
Your soul will breathe ease
—August 2022

*J*t is believed by some that The Divine is the greatest source of love and joy in our lives, that the universe is a manifestation of the Divine, and that there are bridges existing between the spiritual and physical realms.

PRACTICE

- *Read the poem* again, out loud if possible, and in an unrushed way.

- *What most resonates with your spirit today?*

Allow yourself yet another reading of the poem. On this reading, take time to notice what seems less familiar to you. Ask the question between you and Inner Knowing:

- *What could this mean?*

Giving yourself one final reading, close your practice today with this last question:

- *Where will I—might I—can I experience Joy today?*

In the moments of your day that have already passed, and in the moments yet to come, may there be moments of Joy.

DAY 25: LOW AND HIGH VIBRATIONS

What to bring to your practice: *Joy Journal*

When we set our intention towards joy, we will eventually find Joy.

The desire to gain perspective can sometimes come as a result of experiencing an abundance of feelings that are often thought of as "lower frequency feelings," things like jealousy, resentment, anxiety, desperation, unfulfillment, confusion, exhaustion, and the like. (And on the other side of that, things like joy, peace, and love are often thought of as being "higher vibration feelings.")

Now, on one hand, there is absolutely nothing wrong with experiencing the full range of feelings in our lives. In fact, this is ideal!

But for whatever reason, sometimes we can begin to feel stuck in a particular emotion, even when we don't want to be there. For example, feeling panic is an entirely expected way to feel when the car in front of us has suddenly slammed on the brakes and we need to do the same. But if our heart is still beating wildly an hour after the event, that is less than desirable. The same can be true with feelings that occur along the lines of anger or sadness. They can be harmful if we hold them too long.

And so today, we're engaging in the practice of gaining perspective. We want to practice now so that later, when we begin to feel stuck in those lower vibration emotions, we will have the ability to notice it and move into a space where we can access connection to Joy.

PRACTICE

And so to begin, allow yourself a moment of focus, breathing in, breathing out, finding a place of center here in this present moment. Take a couple of these centering breaths, simply saying to yourself: *Breathing in. Breathing out.*

When you feel ready, consider the questions below:

- *Are there any emotions I have felt stuck in lately?*
- *If yes, what use have these emotions served for me?*
- *Do I have a part to play in these emotions I'm feeling?*
- *Is it possible for me to let go of these emotions now?*
- *Is there a way for me to use the energy of these emotions for good?*
- *What have I discovered today?*

Note: If, by some chance, life has been going very well for you, perhaps it would still serve to ask these very same questions. Remember, when we set our intentions towards joy, we eventually find Joy.

DAY 26: ADDING JOYFUL WORDS

A NOTICING PRACTICE

What to bring to your practice: *Your environment & your senses*

~

I once told someone:
"The combination of flavors in this salad is so lovely."

The person replied:
"Are you serious? I can't tell if you're being sarcastic or if you mean it."

*H*aving feelings, including the feeling of joy, can lead to feeling something else: vulnerable. Trying to feel good is risky business. What's to stop something from coming in and stealing our joy? And indeed, all emotions are actually fleeting. And so if we try to cling to joy as an emotion, eventually, it will slip away from us.

But when we connect with Joy as the unlimited essence of our being, the emotion becomes something more: It becomes a part of our lifestyle, which is quite a bit less slippery.

…And yet, there is still struggle because, as a society, many of us have become accustomed to "toning ourselves down." Our world has become so void of delight that we may not even believe one another when we express our emanations of joy. We end up saying, *"Are you serious? I can't tell if you're being sarcastic or if you really mean it."*

PRACTICE

Our spiritual practice for today is all about the exploration of your senses.

Begin by centering yourself here in this moment, taking in a deep, full, life-giving inhale and then sighing into your exhale with great relief as tension and heaviness leave your body.

When you are ready, begin to breathe normally again, allowing your awareness to be fully here. Today, we are engaging the spiritual practice of *adding joyful words* to our lives, words like: Fantastic, Splendid, Wonderful, Fabulous, Sublime, Lovely, Gorgeous…

- "This chair feels *amazingly* comfortable."
- "The sunshine is *divinely* warm."
- "The combination of flavors in this salad is so *lovely.*"

This practice is all about giving voice to what we're noticing. Rather than allowing a joyful moment to pass us by, we're taking the time to actually see it, feel it, taste it—to experience it—because yes, this simply delicious moment is going to pass into many other moments today. The beauty of this moment is that it is a uniquely beautiful moment. Give voice to it. Enjoy it. Try this now in whatever way you can…and if possible, offer yourself several pauses like this one throughout your day.

DAY 27: FINDING PERSPECTIVE

What to bring to your practice: *Joy Song, comfortable space, Joy Journal (optional)*

When perspective widens, so does possibility.

*T*oday we are going to explore the topic of perspective through the lens of movement and music. Don't forget to have your Joy Song cued up and ready to go.

As we usually do, begin by returning to the breath, allowing it to be an anchor for you, bringing you fully into the present moment.

PRACTICE

While here, consider if there is anything in your life that stands out as *needing a wider perspective*—something that could use a little creativity or compassion. It could be a question you've been having, an ongoing relational dynamic, a problem you've been trying to solve...anything at all.

If something comes to mind, perhaps this can become the focus of your practice today. If nothing comes to mind, this is okay, too. Offering ourselves the *practice of perspective* in the more general sense is enough for now.

Having chosen your focus, allow the music to play. Allow the body and music to move together, whether this looks like swaying with the music, rising to your feet, or something else still. The idea here is that music has the ability to move us, to shift us, to take us from one place to another. You may notice a desire to offer more movement in one moment and quite a bit less in another. All of this belongs.

When the song has finished, if you feel there is more to explore, you may wish to play the song again. Whenever your movement feels complete, give yourself a moment of stillness in order to ask:

- *What did I notice?*
- *Did I sense anything?*
- *Did I learn anything?*
- *Has my perspective shifted in any way?*

(Be gentle with these questions. Sometimes we sense something in the moment and sometimes our journey continues to play out in ways that feel hardly perceptible at first while making much more sense in hindsight.) If there are things you'd like to note, consider adding them to your journal.

DAY 28: THE DARK AND THE LIGHT

What to bring to your practice: *Real life, Joy Journal (optional)*

Within the difficulties there is often a gift.

Throughout these last several days, we've been exploring joy through the lens of reframing and perspective. Give yourself a huge round of applause. You've done some hard work this week!

On Day 15 of our Joy Journey, we heard that *Joy is what happens when we can hold both the difficult and the good.*

Now today we hear this: *Within the difficult, there is often a gift.* In sitting with this idea, offer yourself the space to become curious. On one hand, we cannot ignore the importance of naming whatever it is that is actually feeling difficult for us.

The struggle, however, begins to arise when we give in to the temptation to stop at naming the difficult rather than continuing on to engage the wider story. Oftentimes, both loss and gain are present at the exact same time.

To choose not to truly acknowledge our loss is what we sometimes call "toxic positivity," which is not our intention. Rather, we are learning to remember that balance is always, and at all times, about the realness of both things in our lives.

PRACTICE

And so our spiritual practice for today is to offer ourselves the poetic experience of *naming a "dark" and a "light"* in our lives, and *then* to simultaneously *hold both* of those things with compassion and care. We might say:

- Because of school being out, the kids have extra needs this week. This is difficult. But! I also get to wake up a half hour later every day this week, and I'm really thankful for that.
- We forgot to put the leftovers away last night. I'm feeling really irritated about that. At the same time, the kids are really going to enjoy getting mac n cheese for lunch. And in fact, I'm looking forward to seeing their faces light up when they find out.

Offer yourself as many of these as you'd like and as usual, return to this practice of naming your struggle *and* your celebration whenever it feels helpful.

WEEK 5

RENEWAL

DAY 29: RENEWAL THROUGH DISCERNMENT

What to bring to your practice: *Joy Journal*

To live is to become.

*A*s we enter into the 5th week of our Joy Journey, we turn our attention towards the topic of renewal.

Renewal is often the thing we refer to when we are feeling worn out, and, in fact, many *"re"* words could be used to help us describe the experience of bringing vitality back into our being—words like *"refresh"* and *"restore."*

Spiritually speaking, we may wish to think of the renewal process as being a daily, internal experience. But it is also possible to engage in shorter periods of intentional and more intense immersion—a weekend getaway, a day retreat, an afternoon with art supplies and coffee, a walk in the park...

PRACTICE

As we begin our journey with renewal today, borrowing from the Ignatian tradition, we're going to give ourselves the gift of a *check-in*, asking ourselves two simple questions:

- *What is bringing me life?*
- *What is taking life from me?*

But before you begin, as usual, offer yourself a number of centering breaths, giving yourself permission to be fully here, in this moment, becoming more completely aware of your surroundings.

When your body and mind feel calm, answer the two questions above, knowing that all that is to be done today is to simply notice. When you are ready, close your practice by offering yourself a moment of Loving Kindness:

> *May I be happy.*
> *May I be healthy.*
> *May I be strong.*
> *May I be at ease.*

DAY 30: RENEWAL THROUGH DIVINA

What to bring to your practice: *Joy Journal*

WHO KNEW
Who knew, when we moved
We'd remember how air smells
And marvel at birds

Who knew, when we moved
We'd delight at trees dancing
And see them as friends

Who knew, when we moved
We'd snuggle under lightning
And stroll with fireflies
—August 2022

*W*elcome to Day 30! We pause on this day to celebrate the fact that we've been on this journey together for a month now. We are meaningfully past the 21 days it takes to establish a habit and are well on our way to cultivating a lifestyle of joy. Congratulations!

We return our attention today to the topic of renewal. By now we are well familiar with the idea that Joy is the *unlimited essence of our being*, a River that flows through us, a never-ending Wellspring that we can tap into at any time.

PRACTICE

As we read the words above, consider how the concept of renewal is present. In reading these three stanzas above once again, ask yourself:

- *What words are standing out to me today?*

Whatever words or phrases are touching you today, repeat them again, saying them several times over, allowing them to take on even more meaning in your heart.

…After a little while ask the question:

- *Why might these be the words that are standing out to me today?*

What particular meaning do these words hold in connection to your life, your thoughts, your feelings? Why do these words feel particularly special to you today?

…Having sat with whatever has emerged for you, also consider:

- *Do I sense any particular message or desire for action emerging?*

This could be along the lines of spiritual wisdom. Or it could be that there is something you want to do or to change. In asking this question, it can be helpful to remember that all of this is possible, and yet none of this is required.

…Read the three stanzas above one last time, asking the question:

- *What do I want to take with me as I leave my practice today?*

…Whenever your discernment is complete, close your practice by again offering yourself a moment of Loving Kindness:

> *May I be happy.*
> *May I be healthy.*
> *May I be strong.*
> *May I be at ease.*

DAY 31: RENEWAL THROUGH NATURE

What to bring to your practice: *Joy Journal, going outdoors (optional)*

Flowers offer us a wealth of inspiration.

Throughout this week, we've been exploring the subject of Renewal by way of engaging in the spiritual practice of discernment. Today, we continue this theme, allowing our source of inspiration to come from the image of a flower.

May 2023.

PRACTICE

Using the image above, or some other image of your choice, or by getting outside and sitting with actual plant life, take some time with the following questions:

- *What emotion(s) does this image evoke in you?*
- *What does this image stir, or bring forth, in you?*
- *Is there any action or particular message coming up for you?*

When your discernment is complete, close your practice, once again, by offering yourself a moment of Loving Kindness:

> *May I be happy.*
> *May I be healthy.*
> *May I be strong.*
> *May I be at ease.*

DAY 32: RENEWAL THROUGH LETTING GO

What to bring to your practice: *Joy Journal*

Sometimes it's about enjoying the moment...
and then passing into the next moment.

*L*ife is full of seasons, of things that are beginning, things that are in full swing, and things that are transitioning. At times, we can understand and even appreciate this fact. We may even take comfort in knowing that many of the beautiful firsts we experience in life will come again in their own unique ways:

- The emergence of tree buds
- The brilliance of summer blooms
- The splendor of autumn leaves
- The glitter of first snows

But at other times, we lack such clarity, stumbling about as we try to incorporate the loss of our loved ones or accept the realities of a broken family heirloom…

The ability to experience inward renewal on a daily basis turns out to be intimately connected with our ability to accept the transitory nature of our being, to engage the spiritual practice of "letting go."

Earlier this week, we asked ourselves: *What is bringing me life* and *what is taking life from me?*

If we begin to regularly ask ourselves these questions, we will eventually discover that something which was once bringing us life may become something that is now sucking the life out of us.

PRACTICE

And so today, we engage in the spiritual practice of *Letting Go*. To do this, we begin by coming back to our two questions from Day 29:

- *What is bringing me life?*
- *What is taking life from me?*

In answering these questions, pause within yourself in order to notice any emotions, thoughts, or actions that might accompany your answers.

- *Is there anything I can let go of?*

When your practice feels complete, offer yourself a moment of Loving Kindness:

> *May I be happy.*
> *May I be healthy.*
> *May I be strong.*
> *May I be at ease.*

DAY 33: RENEWAL THROUGH YOUR SENSES

What to bring to your practice: *Your surroundings, real life, Joy Journal*

When life feels unpredictable, the natural rhythms of the earth can help.

hroughout this week, we've been taking time to consider the possibility for daily, inward renewal—the ability to draw from an inner wellspring of Joy as our source of restoration. The concept of renewal gives us the ability to begin and begin again, over and over, multiple times a day.

Many of us struggle to maintain our connections to the natural rhythms of life. Lights allow us to work well into the night. Refrigeration and other developments have lessened our dependency on the rhythms of our planet to provide for us. And yet, when we take the time to pause and become aware of them, those natural rhythms can still thrill us, connect us, and even teach us.

PRACTICE

And so, regardless of what season you are currently living in, we pause today for a time of reflection. Offer yourself a centering breath, and then consider for yourself, in this current season in which you are living:

- *What can I enjoy in this moment now?*

(As your answer comes to mind, use your senses to really soak it in.)

- *Now that you're thinking about it, what are 5 good things you can experience in this particular season?*

(Once again, allow your senses to become involved in this experience.)

- *Name something that is either bringing you renewal or that could contribute to your renewal.*

When your discernment is complete, close your practice today with an offering of Loving Kindness towards yourself:

> *May I be happy.*
> *May I be healthy.*
> *May I be strong.*
> *May I be at ease.*

DAY 34: RENEWAL THROUGH MOVEMENT

What to bring to your practice: Joy Journal
Optional: Art supplies, space to move, outdoors, camera, Joy Song, etc.

Oh the joy of a spiral found in nature!

A t times, our experience of Joy involves a journey inward, a chance to draw from a limitless interior well. That said, we often access that inner well by connecting with something more externally tangible, in this case, we offer attention to spirals and S-curves as they relate symbolically to notions of growth, transformation, and renewal.

As we seek a few moments of daily renewal today, consider one of the three practices below, or, if you'd prefer, modify one in a way that will serve you. In whatever you choose, may this be an enriching time of renewal for you:

April 2024.

PRACTICE

1. *Grab a blank piece of paper and some crayons, colored pencils, pens, or paints. Create your own S-Curve masterpiece.*
2. *Turn on some music and create your own interpretive dance, incorporating turns and spirals as you go.*
3. *Take to the outdoors in search of spirals and S-curves, photographing them if the inspiration strikes.*

At the end of your practice, close with a moment of Loving Kindness towards yourself:

> *May I be happy.*
> *May I be healthy.*
> *May I be strong.*
> *May I be at ease.*

DAY 35: RENEWAL THROUGH CELEBRATING JOURNEY

What to bring to your practice: *Joy Journal*

It's amazing what can come from a teeny tiny little seed.

*D*o you know what day it is? It's celebration day!

Each day this week—and, really, for the last 35 days, you've been planting little seeds in your life—seeds that become large plants!

Now, if you have any experience with seeds, you may already know that some seeds spring up very quickly while others can take so long, you begin to wonder if anything is even going on under that soil. But from the darkness of the quiet soil comes abundant life.

As this week comes to a close, spend a few moments reflecting in your Joy Journal:

PRACTICE

- *What seeds have you planted this week?*
- *What first fruits are you experiencing in your overall journey?*

And then, for one last time this week, close with a moment of Loving Kindness towards yourself:

> *May I be happy.*
> *May I be healthy.*
> *May I be strong.*
> *May I be at ease.*

WEEK 6

TRANSCENDENCE & FORGIVENESS

DAY 36: TAKING A BIRD'S EYE VIEW

What to bring to your practice: *Joy Journal, Joy Song (optional)*

A bird's-eye view brings us to the heart of it all.

Welcome to the 6th week of your Joy Journey experience. Throughout this week, we'll be talking about transcendence, the experience of going beyond, or rising above. This is an important part of our journey as it's a part of what gives our lives meaning and purpose.

Certainly, there are many ways in which we can experience transcendence, but for today, we begin by "taking to the skies."

PRACTICE

As you prepare, you may wish to consider cueing up your Joy Song. And once again, begin by taking a moment to center yourself. It can be tempting to rush through our lives, merely checking things off our to-do list. But in this moment now, breathe deeply and slowly. Allow the edges of your eyes and your mouth to soften, become aware of tension and let it go. Invite Presence. And when you are ready, imagine you are a bird. You may be sitting high up in a tree or soaring through the skies like a majestic eagle. Wherever you are, allow yourself to see the landscape below. What's there? What can you notice from this bird's-eye view?

When you're ready, consider the following question:

- *In what area of my life could I use a "bird's-eye view?"*
- *How does taking this bird's-eye view affect my perspective? My thoughts? My feelings?*

Make note of anything that comes to mind in your Joy Journal.

As you close your practice, offer a blessing of Loving Kindness to yourself and anyone who may have come to mind.

DAY 37: I CAN, AND ALSO

What to bring to your practice: *Joy Journal*

Transcendence is an act of movement.

esterday, we took some time to imagine at least one aspect of our lives from a broader perspective. Today, we take that practice a step further, considering the role that forgiveness has to play in our lives.

In considering a joy-infused life, whether we are speaking of the momentary delights available to us throughout the day, or drawing deeply from the unlimited essence of our being, without the ability to let go, well...the truth of the matter is, we can only go as far as our burdens will allow.

When we take that bird's-eye view, as we did yesterday, it helps us get a fresh perspective on our worries and our relational struggles. The question is: What *are* the worries and disagreements, petty or otherwise, that may be holding us down, preventing us from a fuller experience of transcendence?

In asking this question, something we'll want to keep in mind is that this is a work that can take time, so please be patient and kind with yourself.

PRACTICE

To begin, consider one or more of the following prompts and questions:

- *Conflict:* What conflicts or annoyances do I regularly rehearse in my mind?
- *Unworthiness:* In what ways do I feel I don't "measure up?"
- *Competition:* What am I striving for that's creating irritation in my life?
- *Perfectionism:* What demands am I placing on myself or others that appear to be doing more harm than good?
- *Grudges:* Who do I complain about?
- *Denial:* Is there any feedback I've been given that I just don't want to hear?

In whatever has come up in your list, consider offering yourself an "I can…and also…" statement:

For example, if I said:

- "I am upset that I gained a few pounds over the winter."

Perhaps my "I can…and also…" statement might be something like:

- "I *can* work towards my health goals…*and also* appreciate my overall health."

Or another example. If I said:

- "I've been told that I don't respond well to feedback."

Perhaps my "I can...and also..." statement might be something like:

- *I can* be efficient and effective in my work...*and also* offer flexibility and kindness to my coworkers.

In coming up with a few of these statements, we may begin to discover ways to diminish some of the burden in our lives that can keep us feeling imprisoned. Perhaps we can begin to find a bit of transcendence in our lives instead.

When your practice is complete, offer a blessing of Loving Kindness to yourself and anyone who may have come to mind.

DAY 38: THE SKY AS SPIRITUAL COMPANION

What to bring to your practice: *The sky, Joy Journal*

No matter where you live, the sky is always there.

 o experience infinite wonder, all we have to do is look up.

PRACTICE

Today's spiritual practice is *allowing the sky to become our companion.* Whether this looks like moving to a nearby window or actually heading outside, take some time to look up.

Give yourself a number of moments in this space, trying not to wander to the upcoming events of the day or the things that need to be solved. Surely there will be time for these things. But just for these few moments, allow yourself to simply be with the infinite sky.

November 2022.

- *After a couple of moments, perhaps take some time to write in your Joy Journal, noting what this experience was like for you, what happened, what you noticed.*

When your practice is complete, offer up your gratitude for the ways in which the sky has companioned you today.

DAY 39: OUR WHOLE SELVES

What to bring to your practice: *Joy Journal*

We can't transcend what we won't spend time with.

Today's spiritual practice is to sit with the whole of ourselves. For many of us, we have been given certain messages our entire lives. When we're sad, someone tells us not to cry. When we're angry, someone tells us to calm down. If we're feeling anxious, we're told not to worry. And on it goes.

The good news about emotions is that they're fluid, tending to rise and fall, similar to waves in the ocean. But with that being said, naming and leaving space to feel our emotions is an important part of our life experience. It's what keeps our well-intentioned brains from trying to protect us with small-self solutions.

September 2022.

PRACTICE

And so today, we take a moment to sit with the whole of ourselves.

If you would like, begin first by using the quote and image for today as a way of grounding your practice. Take a moment to breathe slowly and deeply.

- If you are reading the quote, read it slowly several times, allowing yourself to linger on the words as you go.
- If you are looking at the image, scan the image slowly as you breathe, allowing your focus to remain on whatever emerges for you.

After a few moments of pause, take some time with the questions below, answering whichever ones feel most relevant to you or adapting them to fit your circumstances:

Considering my more difficult emotions:

- *What hurts? What am I angry about?*
- *Why does it hurt? Why am I angry*
- *What can help?*

When your practice is complete, return again to either the quote or the image for today. If there is some revelation that has come for you, consider how you will respond to that revelation.

DAY 40: INNER-LIGHT VISUALIZATION

A GUIDED MEDITATION

What to bring to your practice: *A comfortable space*

Light offers us many gifts. Like energy. And transcendence.

*A*s we begin, take a moment to settle into whatever place is supporting you at this moment. You may wish to close your eyes, allowing yourself to become more aware of that part of you that is connected with Divine Presence. Oftentimes we are busy and less connected to this part of our being. But in this moment, we take in a deep breath. And as we exhale, we come into this place where our spirit connects with Divine Spirit. And we rest in the goodness of that space…

…After having taken a few of these centering breaths, begin to imagine a small light that originates at the core of your being. It may be a light that originates in your heart space, or perhaps quite literally at the center of your core. If you'd like, you can even place a hand on that space as you breathe gently in and out, allowing yourself to see this place of light within—this Divine Source of Light within.

Light has a way of breaking through the darkness. As we continue on in this space, imagine this light within you, originating at that center point, and then slowly moving outwards, radiating, moving and filling your entire being with light, a little bit at a time, until it reaches the very edges of your physical self. '

As that light comes to the very edges of you, continue to observe it as it moves beyond you, no longer contained by the space of your body, but radiating out from you and into the world. Extending from you and beyond you…

…Continuing to breathe, return now to the center of this light again. Notice the warming presence that this Light brings to you, filling each and every part of you with a gentle warmth.

Notice the beauty of this light. How lovely it is as it radiates in you, through you, and out from you. Notice what this light means to you.

What, if anything, does this light say to you? Are there any messages for you in regard to who you are and the light that you share with the world?

Love, Strength and Possibility all flow from this light. Remember that you can return to this practice at any time, seeing again this light within that expands to fill your whole body and flow out from you.

As we close today, feel the purpose, peace and possibility that stream from this place. As you take another deep breath, return again to this moment in time, feeling the support of the space that is supporting you and expressing gratitude for this light that shines from the core of your being.

DAY 41: EXPERIENCE THE LIGHTNESS

What to bring to your practice:
A comfortable space, Joy Song. Joy Journal (optional)

*To be truly free, we must eventually part ways
with that which leaves us bitter.*

Sitting still is definitely an important part of overall health. But so is movement. And so for today's spiritual practice, we once again cue up our Joy Song.

PRACTICE

After considering this idea that to be free we must eventually part ways with that which leaves us bitter, allow the song to play. And as it plays, rather than merely listening to it, allow your body to move with the music, connecting with this notion of upward movement. Be as creative as you'd like, taking note of any responses you might have. After all, if joy is the unlimited essence of our being, then it's merely a matter of connecting, and connecting again, to that limitless well. Play the song as many times as you'd like until your practice feels complete.

Rather than moving on too quickly, take some time to check in with yourself.

- *What do I notice physically? Emotionally? Mentally? Spiritually?*
- *What comes to mind for me and why?*
- *Are there any actions I want to take as I move on with my day?*

DAY 42: ENJOYING YOUR WELLSPRING

What to bring to your practice: *Joy Journal*

The secret to a joyful life is sometimes as simple as choosing to lighten up.

Throughout these last 7 days, you've offered yourself the opportunity to look at your life from a bird's-eye view, to look up and see beyond those details in the day that can seem to take over, and you've allowed yourself to embrace this notion of transcendence with your whole self.

As this week comes to a close, offer yourself a few moments of reflection. If you'd like, use the questions below to aid your practice:

PRACTICE

- *In what way did I lighten up this week? And when I did, what happened?*
- *What experience (spiritual or otherwise) can I celebrate this week?*

Take a moment to celebrate your journey today. Offer yourself a treat. Enjoy this wellspring of Joy within you!

WEEK 7

GENEROSITY & KINDNESS

DAY 43: THREE FORMS OF GENEROSITY

What to bring to your practice: *Joy Journal*

Generosity and kindness create quick connections to Joy.

Welcome to Week 7 of our Joy Journey! This week, we are reflecting on generosity and kindness as paths that help us to draw deeply from the wellspring of Joy within.

One way to think about generosity is to break it up into three categories as is done in the Buddhist tradition. We can choose to give:

- *Materially:* Donating things and money
- *Courageously:* Offering protection, counsel or solace
- *Compassionately:* Offering comfort or wisdom

Acts of kindness and generosity are simple ways to make people feel good because when we do these things, our brains release the chemical oxytocin. This chemical is what creates in us a desire to bond. It's the reason we experience friendship and love.

And one of the best things about oxytocin is that, when we do something nice for another person—with no expectations of reciprocity—not only do we receive that surge of oxytocin, but so does the person we have helped, and anyone else who witnesses the act as well. Also, a little fun fact: The more oxytocin we have in our bodies, the more generous we become. (Learn more about this in Simon Sinek's talk, *The Scientific Power of Kindness.*)

To give an example:

Say we're in a public space and we see a small child trying to reach something that's too high for them. We observe that as they are reaching and struggling, an older woman sees what's happening and instinctively reaches out to lift the child up. We instinctively say to ourselves, "Oh, look. What an endearing sight, this older woman reaching out to help this little child."

But then, as we continue to watch, we see that this isn't going to work. The older woman lacks the strength to hold the child up long enough for the child to reach. We start to become worried. But before we can do anything about it, yet another woman rushes over to help lift the little child up. The two women work together, and the child achieves their goal.

In this very basic, yet very meaningful interaction, everyone involved benefits from a little release of oxytocin, which is such a big deal because we humans really thrive on connection.

These feelings of connection make us want to be kind and generous again so that we can feel that way again. And on it goes, the cycle repeating itself over and over again…unless, of course, we experience a break in this chain of events for too long, in which case, all that is needed is to start the chain back up again by doing or witnessing some act of kindness or generosity.

PRACTICE

Having read these words, take a moment to return to stillness, allowing your breathing to slow and your thoughts to fade for a moment. When you are ready, ask yourself:

- *What intentions do I want to set for my day?*

Return to this question throughout the day whenever you'd like.

DAY 44: SEVEN WAYS TO BE GENEROUS

What to bring to your practice: *Joy Journal*

There is power in your loving and your giving.

*A*s we continue exploring generosity and kindness this week, doing so as a way to access the wellspring of Joy within, it's important to continuously remind ourselves of the many ways that we can be generous.

We can be generous with our:

- *Thoughts:* Considering those around us with unconditional positive regard
- *Words:* Building one another up rather than tearing each other down
- *Money:* Investing and sharing our gifts

- *Time:* Offering our hands and feet to cocreate goodness in our world
- *Things:* Sharing what we have and bridging the gaps created by need
- *Influence:* Spreading the ethic of love, peace, joy and beyond
- *Attention:* Communicating the preciousness of the one who is in front of us

PRACTICE

In considering these many ways of being generous in our world, allow yourself to sit contemplatively with the following ideas:

There is someone in the world right now

…who is feeling hopeless
…who doesn't know where to go or what to do
…who longs for love
…who needs a trustworthy friend

And also, there is power

…in our giving
…in our love

When you are ready, continue on to the Reflection Prompts below:

- *What inspirations arise for you?*
- *What intentions do you want to set for your day?*

As you close your practice today, may the Divine Spark within continue to open your heart wherever you go.

DAY 45: THE PARADOX OF GENEROSITY

What to bring to your practice: *Joy Journal*

In the natural world, we find ourselves surrounded by Joy.

*G*enerosity and kindness can extend not only to other humans in our world but to all living beings and things. And what's more, while it can sometimes be another person's actions that inspire us, it is equally possible for another living being or thing to ignite that internal spark.

PRACTICE

And so for today, we turn our attention to the wisdom of nature, leaving space for the words below:

Dear Mother Nature
How generously you give
Life comes from your touch

We come home to you
We feast on the fruits of you
We draw life from you

You show us the way
How to be, and be again,
Even in changing

My cup overflows
To the point that I must ask:
How can I help you?

As you consider these words…

- *What words feel like wisdom for your soul today?*
- *What inspirations do you notice emerging?*
- *What intentions do you want to set for your day?*

May there be goodness in your life and the lives of those you touch today.

DAY 46: CONSIDERING THE COMMUNITY

What to bring to your practice: *Joy Journal*

Compassionate social activism requires us to fully embody ourselves.

*A*s we continue exploring generosity and kindness this week as ways to engage the deep wellspring of Joy within, what you may have begun to notice, or may have known for quite some time now, is that joy is something we can embody. We can give joy a tangible and visible expression. Joy is a part of us and we are a part of Joy.

How this looks from one moment and one day to the next, however, is not always the same. On some days, we come with great elation. On other days, we come with great service. It all depends on what the moment calls for. But one way that we can embody Joy is through our service, by engaging in our communities, continually seeking to bring about just treatment for all.

And so, in considering that social action requires us to fully embody ourselves:

PRACTICE

- *What do you relate to?*
- *What might it look like to "realize a more just world?"*
- *How have you seen these themes embodied in the past?*
- *In what ways do you feel inspired to embody generosity and kindness?*

As you go through your day today, may the Divine interconnectedness of all things bring you great joy.

DAY 47: SMILE!

What to bring to your practice: *Your smile, Joy Journal (optional)*

Smile! Notice how it changes the quality of your interactions.

esterday we spoke about embodying the Joy that exists within us. Today we continue this beautiful act of embodiment by embracing the gift of smiling. The benefits of smiling have been well-documented. We talked earlier this week about how acts of kindness release the chemical oxytocin in our brains. As a quick Google search will reveal, smiling, as it turns out...just the simple act of smiling...reduces stress through the release of neuropeptides and reduces both physical and emotional pain through the release of neurotransmitters.

And these are just the personal benefits! When we smile at others, their bodies offer them a similar experience, which isn't all that surprising in light of our conversation yesterday about the interconnectedness of all things. But even if these things aren't that surprising when we think about it, they sure are remarkable!

And so for today, our spiritual practice is simple: Smile.

PRACTICE, PART I

Begin by smiling to yourself even now. Allow your breath to center you, and then ever so gently, allow the corners of your mouth to begin to lift. Immediately, you may find that your eyes begin to "smile" as well. Take this smile fully in, embody it and notice what a powerful and inviting thing your smile is.

PRACTICE, PART II

Smile at someone else. With gentle eyes that reflect their preciousness, allow your breath to fill you to the core of your being, becoming fully present as the corners of your mouth begin to lift and take the form of a life-giving smile.

- *As you smile at yourself and others today, what do you notice about yourself physically? Emotionally? Mentally? Spiritually?*

May your day be full of the embodied smile and may it break open the floodgates of Joy both in your life and in the lives of those you touch.

DAY 48: POUR OUT LIGHT

What to bring to your practice: *Joy Journal*

I'M JUST SO SORRY
I didn't hold you
In fact, I criticized you
I'm just so sorry
—September 2022

REFLECT PRECIOUSNESS
Reflect preciousness
Look in their eyes and see light
Get caught up in love.
—August 2022

PRACTICE

*T*oday's practice invites us to put one thing on our to-do list today:

- Let your light pour generously upon all things

As we consider the words of these poems:

- *In what ways do the words of the haikus above resonate today?*
- *Who are the precious beings in your life?*
- *Take a moment to offer a prayer of Loving Kindness for these beings:*

    May they be happy.
    May they be safe.
    May they be healthy.
    May they be at ease.

- *In what other ways might you want to pour out light today?*

May Light flow to you, from you, and back again. And may it be the Joy of your heart.

DAY 49: JOY MULTIPLIED THROUGH SHARING

What to bring to your practice: *Your Story*

Amplify your joy by sharing it with another.

oday we celebrate all that we have experienced over the last 7 days. We've spoken a lot this week about how embodying joy through generosity and kindness can create the possibility for more joy in our lives.

We have shared ourselves, our gifts, our time, our attention, and more with others, which, in turn, has opened the door for yet more Light to flow in us and in the world around us.

But because life can be busy—and because we are very often prone to offering our attention to, and remembering, that which has been difficult, frustrating, and annoying in our lives—we need moments to really savor that which has been good.

PRACTICE

And so for today, we take a moment to reflect:

- *What good has come from my spiritual practices this week?*

As you prepare to go about the rest of your day:

- *Share your experience(s) of joy with someone else.*

Tell someone—anyone! Because sharing our joy has a way of bringing joy to others. Happy joy sharing!

WEEK 8

PLAY

DAY 50: THE JOY OF PLAY

What to bring to your practice: *Joy Journal*

GUILT-FREE ENJOYMENT
Don't want to be used.
Don't take advantage of me...
Because I'll do it!

I'll do all your work.
While you're still sleeping I will!
But I won't have lived.

I need space to breathe
I need to savor today
Guilt-free enjoyment
—August 2022

*A*s we enter our 8th week in our Joy Journey, with so much foundation beneath us, we turn our attention to Play.

Adults can sometimes struggle with play. We become entrenched in the things that need to be done, the demands, the responsibilities… Many of us report even struggling to have a desire to play. But the research tells us that play will increase our overall wellbeing, allowing us to feel healthier in every aspect of living—mentally, emotionally, physically, and even spiritually.

If we want to live a life of joy, we need play. And specifically, we need play that we enjoy, which can take some figuring out. It takes asking ourselves: Now that I think about it, what type of play do I enjoy?

The statements below may help you to identify what sorts of things feel like play to you. Read each one, taking note of which ones ring particularly true in your innermost being.

PRACTICE

- *I enjoy collecting, whether it be things or information.*
- *I love the thrill of a good competition.*
- *I lose myself in creative projects.*
- *It's exhilarating to plan big events.*
- *I light up at the thought of a great adventure.*
- *I seek out jokes to share with others.*
- *I choose movement whenever possible.*
- *I immerse myself in imagination and stories.*

Having taken time to identify the statements that feel most true for you, return to today's poem on guilt-free enjoyment.

- *Consider again which of the statements above resonate with the core of your being.*

- *Or...what statements came to mind that felt like the core of your being.*

As our exploration of play begins, consider setting an intention to offer yourself moments of play throughout your days. Notice which lines from today's poem resonate with you, and consider how you might allow them to come alive in your lived experience.

DAY 51: COMING ALIVE

What to bring to your practice: *Joy Journal*

Doing things out of obligation is a great way to kill your joy.
Doing things because they light you up...bring on the joy!

esterday, we began exploring the idea that creativity is a skill that can be developed through the medium of play. You'll recall, we also noted that creativity is an important component in improving our sense of wellbeing. When employed intentionally, creativity serves to aid us in our pursuit of growth, meaning, and purpose.

Regardless of the stage of life we may be living in, we often need creativity in order to solve problems, to help us see "the big picture," and to overcome either/or paradigms that may not serve our partic-ular situations. But, of course, when things don't happen the way we want them to, any number of emotions can arise. To use the words we find in the Buddhist tradition, we experience suffering.

In order to feel that sense of thriving, while it can sometimes be helpful to employ things like "holy indifference" and "letting go," it can also be helpful to engage our creative side, to ask ourselves, "If not this way, is there some other solution or possibility?"

The truth of the matter is: You are an individual, a person with unique gifts, callings, and purposes. There are things that light you up and make you excited to be alive. The more time you can spend doing these things, the more you will feel that sense of meaning and purpose.

In yesterday's spiritual practice, you took time to identify the special-to-you ways in which you bring fun and play into your life.

PRACTICE

Today, our practice involves *asking ourselves what lights us up*. Begin by using your centering and grounding practices, allowing your mind and body to become still enough to connect with the Wisdom within. Breathe slowly, arriving here in this present moment. And then, when you are ready, ask yourself:

- *What lights you up and makes you come alive?*

…And now that you've asked that question, another question:

- *When you are doing that, what specifically makes you happy?*

…And then just one more question:

- *Where else could you experience that happiness in your life?*

This is an important question because what you love may be accessible to you in numerous ways.

May asking these questions help you to come alive today and inspire your path as you pursue a joy-filled life.

DAY 52: EMBODYING WONDER

What to bring to your practice: *A camera, your environment*

Joy comes when we see in Divine ways.

PRACTICE

- *Take a picture*

As we continue our exploration of creativity, your spiritual practice for today is simple. Find something in your environment that inspires your sense of creativity and take a picture of it. Maybe even consider going outdoors and allowing nature to become your teacher. When you've found whatever it is you'd like to capture, you're welcome to share that picture with others or to keep it to yourself. But our practice for today is about *allowing wonder to become a part of your natural way of being.*

- *What captures you? What makes you curious? What brings you to a place of exploration?*

Today is about embodying the experience of play and wonder. It's about looking beyond your ordinary ways of seeing. May you find the Divine in far more places today than you would have expected, and may it bring you great fullness of joy!

DAY 53: LAUGHTER

What to bring to your practice: *Your sense of humor*

When life gives you a dumpster fire, find a way to laugh.

$\mathcal{A}$s we continue our exploration of play as it connects to increasing our quality of life in a joy-filled context, today we turn our attention to the subject of laughter. As with all things, how naturally predisposed we are towards laughter is going to vary from person to person. But being able to accept our lives as they are, even as we work for change, really does help us to feel more *joy-full*.

PRACTICE

- *Laughter*

To begin, sometimes it can be helpful to warm up the ole laughter engine. Begin by imagining something that would be mildly amusing to you. If you can't think of anything, how about this:

Q: What did the pirate say when he turned 80?
A: *"Aye matey."*

Or how about this?

Knock, knock.
Who's there?
Howl.
Howl who?
Howl you know unless you open the door?

...And now that we've (hopefully) warmed up the laughter engine a bit...

Did you know that there's this thing called Laughter Yoga? If you don't believe me, look it up. There are plenty of videos you could check out on the subject.

To give it a try:

Start by brushing off your shoulders, shooing away all the judgment that weighs you down day in and day out. Once you've done that, begin clapping your hands to a beat, maybe like so:

Slow—Slow—Fast—Fast—Fast (repeat)

As you do this, say these syllables aloud:

Ho—Ho—Hee—Hee—Ha

(This may seem funny, but when you engage in laughter, the body will follow suit, and you will start to feel the emotion connected to laughter, which decreases the cortisol in your body while increasing endorphins.)

Now, once again, trying not to take yourself too seriously...

Return to your clapping while saying the words:

Ho—Ho—Hee—Hee—Ha

Allow the laughter within to emerge again.

When your laughter is complete, bring the hands to heart's center:

> Inhale—*I am strong*
> Exhale—*I am healthy*
> (Repeat a couple more times)

- *As you prepare to close your practice today, set an intention to add a little bit of laughter into the rest of your day.*

Happy laughing! :)

DAY 54: PLAYING WITH CIRCLES

What to bring to your practice: *Joy Song, Joy Journal*
Optional: Colored pencils, crayons, markers, etc.

The circle is symbolic of so many things: movement, life, endlessness, equity.
Today we add joy to the list of things symbolized by the circle.

When it comes to living into a practice of play, there are certain ways in which we can, well, get the ball rolling. Yesterday we did this by allowing ourselves permission to laugh, even in the middle of our more difficult moments.

Today, we do this by incorporating the circle into our spiritual practice. Circles have very powerful roles in our lives. For instance, without them, we wouldn't have wheels. But we may also take for granted that many sources of play come in the shape of a circle—basketballs, bubbles, frisbees, hula hoops...If you're a *Lord of the Rings* fan, consider hobbits who turn out to be some of the happiest characters in the story. And look at that—circle-shaped windows and doors!

The fact that circles represent a brighter disposition is, perhaps, natural intuition. Baby faces are predominantly round faces. And what do we all say about babies? "Awww, look at that cute baby!" When people get married, we often engage in a ritual of exchanging wedding rings, rings that come in the shape of a circle, symbolizing an infinite, unending love. When we want to have a meeting where all people are considered equal, what configuration do we sit in? A circle! Circles are chock full of meaning!

PRACTICE

And so today, we bring the circle into our spiritual practice, allowing ourselves to play with whatever meaning the circle might help us uncover today. To begin, start by putting your Joy Song on repeat. As the song plays, draw a big circle on a page of your Joy Journal, or maybe draw yourself a number of circles on that page.

While your Joy Song is playing, allow it to help you transition to this moment now, opening your awareness to Presence. If you'd like, you're welcome to doodle or jot words down on the page. But it may be helpful to simply sit and breathe as the song plays.

Once the song has finished, if you'd like, you can play the song again, playing with this theme of circles on the page. Or, you could also choose to simply allow the memory of the song to be there as you spend some time interacting on the page in creative ways.

- *As your practice comes to a close, set your intention to notice how circles connect meaningfully in your day-to-day life.*

DAY 55: PLAY THROUGH MUSIC

What to bring to your practice: *Joy Song, a comfortable space*

If we want to pass on joy to others, we will have to first embody it ourselves.

*W*e began this week with a poem called "Guilt-free Enjoyment" which talked about our deep need for time and space to breathe and savor so that we could enjoy our lives free of guilt.

Throughout this week, we have been embracing play as a spiritual practice, offering ourselves the freedom to embody joy and to explore the world through the lens of a creative and wondering spirit.

Today we offer ourselves one more chance to embody play, to interact with the simple joys all around us through the inspiration of song. (It's time to once again cue up your Joy Song!)

PRACTICE

To begin, play the song, allowing yourself to simply take in the words and any images that may come to mind. As always, our journey begins by allowing ourselves to be fully present, fully here.

Once the song has finished, take a moment to breathe slowly, offering yourself a couple of life-giving breaths, connecting to the Light within.

When you're ready, play the song a 2nd time, this time, allowing yourself to embody the song in a way that feels right to you. This may mean swaying gently in your seat. Or, you may feel the desire to get up and allow your entire body to move. Whatever you choose, allow the story to be told through your movement. Perhaps even try creating a makeshift drum and becoming a part of the band. It's all up to you.

When your practice is complete, ask the question:

- *What has come up for me today that I want to take with me into the rest of my day?*

DAY 56: CELEBRATING THE EMERGING JOY

What to bring to your practice: *Joy Journal*

Actively celebrate those moments when you realize you're seeing things from a new perspective.

Today is your day to celebrate that you, despite the lists, the shoulds, and the ought-to's, have taken time to allow joy into your life through the act of play. Some of the things you've been invited into this week may have come more naturally to you than others. This is okay. For many of us, we get into a bit of a routine, and over time, our routines can end up feeling less vibrant than they once did. Changing things up can be an effective (and proven) strategy for seeing things with a new perspective.

At times, that newness comes by way of shifting our environment. At other times, we may be helped by doing something different with our behavior. But whatever way these things happen, changing our routine can be a catalyst for helping us engage with a renewed heart and fresh eyes.

PRACTICE

As we bring our week of play to a close, first take a moment to applaud yourself if you tried something different this week. And then, ask yourself:

- *What new insights, ideas, or revelations have I had this week?*

And if you'd like, you can also ask yourself:

- *How have I experienced Divine Presence this week?*

May you be well today.

WEEK 9

LOVE & COMPASSION

DAY 57: EXTENDING LOVE

What to bring to your practice: *Joy Journal*

People don't have to be down and out before we offer them love and care.

Welcome to the 9th week of our Joy Journey! Our theme for this week is Love and Compassion. By now, you've probably realized that spending time connecting to the positive in your life goes a long way toward increasing your sense of wellbeing. And in some ways, that seems easy enough, right? Think positive thoughts, surround yourself with things you enjoy...and...boom! Wellbeing improves!

But what most of us very quickly come to realize is that difficulty and stress are inescapable. Our wellbeing needs something powerful enough to help us weather the totality of our lives. What's more, we need practices that we can engage in while we're in the midst of our very real and very active lives. And so this week, we're honing in on some age-old wisdom:

> *The fastest way to a positive mental state*
> *is love and compassion.*

And in truth, we've been sprinkling this idea into our Joy Journey for a while now. In Week 5 we were invited to offer a blessing of Loving Kindness to ourselves:

> *May I be happy.*
> *May I be healthy.*
> *May I be strong.*
> *May I be at ease.*

We took time to focus on the self during that week because offering love and compassion to others begins with an ability to, first, be loving and kind to ourselves. This week, however, we expand on these themes, allowing our light to extend beyond the self and into the world around us.

PRACTICE

Today's practice involves offering Loving Kindness to others:

> *May you be well*

Do you ever find yourself in a room with others, and yet, seemingly in your own world? Though it's very easy to lose our sense of mindful connection, when it comes to joy, this ability to become increasingly present really goes a long way.

To do this practice: Anywhere you find yourself in the presence of one or more people, begin by inhaling and becoming aware of their presence in some meaningful way. This inhale moment is all about really seeing them.

And then as you exhale, silently say the words:

May you be well.

If there are others in the room, you may want to keep the practice going as you continue breathing, seeing each one of them on the inhale and then silently offering these words of blessing on the exhale.

Now that you've read about this practice, take some time to ask yourself:

- *How might I incorporate these ideas into my life today?*

When your reflection is complete, close your practice by offering someone you care about a moment of Loving Kindness:

May you be happy.
May you be healthy.
May you be strong.
May you be at ease.

DAY 58: OUR INTERCONNECTED LIVES

What to bring to your practice: *Joy Journal*

Be interdependent.
Because, truthfully, you already are.

estern culture, as you may be well aware, is incredibly individualistic. From adolescence on, we encounter moments of being assessed by the numbers. We're told many times over to discover what makes us unique and to allow that uniqueness to help us forge a path forward. This isn't to say that we haven't also been encouraged towards love and compassion. But for most of us, the joy that comes from seeing ourselves as interdependent has been highly underemphasized.

Consider for a moment, an exchange we had with some trees in our yard:

We had moved into a new home—a corner lot in a rural town that was miles away from the hustle and bustle of the city we had once called home. As we settled into this new place, we found ourselves surrounded by all kinds of "new." Wasp nests above the garage—new. Rain in July? New! Japanese beetles eating all the leaves off the birch trees...so...new.

At the same time, I found myself in a training course that was introducing me to Indigenous wisdom. It had never occurred to me to talk to water or bless the trees or give offerings to the harvest before removing it from the ground. I was learning about the interconnectedness of all things, and it was touching me at a core level.

About that same time, it came to our attention that we needed to remove a few trees. This felt like a total betrayal of the new things I was learning. I found myself wondering: *How dare I?!* And: *Isn't this so unfair that someone who had come before me made such "horrible decisions" that were now becoming my responsibility to "fix?!"* Then I remembered this practice of blessing the trees...

As a family, we headed outside, going around to each of the trees, thanking each of them for all they had done and then blessing them in all that they would become as they went forward into the world in a different way.

It was a moment of profound interconnectedness, lingering far beyond that one moment in time. Just as those trees in our yard were and are a part of a much larger whole, engaged in many connections and relationships, all constantly in motion, changing and transforming, day by day and season by season, so it is with us all. Our ability to recognize this interconnectedness, this non-separateness, goes a long way in helping us engage with the practice of Loving Kindness.

To this day, it is my desire to continue to honor the trees we blessed that day, creating and helping to sustain life where we can and honoring life in its many forms all around us.

Having read these words, consider spending some time with your Joy Journals:

PRACTICE

- *What is my initial reaction to hearing that I am an interconnected, non-separate being?*
- *What do I need in order to see the world as it actually is?*
- *How can I see interconnectedness around me right now?*
- *What can I notice arising in me as I name these things?*

When your practice is complete offer a prayer of Loving Kindness to one of these connections in your life:

> *May you be happy.*
> *May you be healthy.*
> *May you be strong.*
> *May you be at ease.*

DAY 59: THE NATURE CONNECTION

What to bring to your practice:
Your natural environment, Joy Journal (optional)

∽

We are not separate from nature—we are a part of it.

Yesterday we took some time to consider the interconnectedness of all things, which included some consideration of how various elements in nature are connected together. Connecting with nature and living beings beyond the more-than-human world is an important part of improving our own sense of grounding, rootedness, and, ultimately, joy. There's a certain miracle of the heart, a change within that occurs when we are able to put ourselves "in the shoes" of the tree, the blade of grass, the insect, and so on.

And so for today's spiritual practice, spend a bit of time with the practice below. (And if today isn't a good day to get outside, feel free to use the picture from the following picture:)

Whitman's Pond, Weymouth, Massachusetts, June 2023.

PRACTICE

1. Step outside.
2. Draw a circle, either literally or with your mind's eye.
3. Consider: What all is inside of that circle?

When your time of discernment is complete, offer a prayer of Loving Kindness to one of these beings that your attention has turned to today:

> *May you be happy.*
> *May you be healthy.*
> *May you be strong.*
> *May you be at ease.*

DAY 60: OUR EMOTIONAL CONNECTION

What to bring to your practice: *Joy Journal*

When we sit compassionately with others, each of us begins to experience personal, transformational, and incomprehensible healing.

Our experience of joy is not separate from our experience of healing. For one, joy can very much make sorrow feel more bearable. But it's equally important to realize that when we do not tend to the wounds within, joy becomes increasingly more difficult to access. Recognizing the ways in which we are all connected, even through pain, can help us find the healing we need in order to access more joy. In other words, even our emotions are interconnected.

Below you'll find the Buddhist Parable "Kisa Gotami and the Mustard Seed."

Read the story slowly, perhaps even more than once.

KISA GOTAMI & THE MUSTARD SEED—A BUDDHIST PARABLE

During Buddha's time, there lived a woman named Kisa Gotami. She married young and gave birth to a son. One day, the baby fell sick and died soon after. Kisa Gotami loved her son greatly and refused to believe that her son was dead. She carried the body of her son around her village, asking if there was anyone who could bring her son back to life.

The villagers all saw that the son was already dead and there was nothing that could be done. They advised her to accept his death and make arrangements for the funeral.

In great grief, she fell upon her knees and clutched her son's body close to her body. She kept uttering for her son to wake up.

A village elder took pity on her and suggested that she consult the Buddha.

"Kisa Gotami. We cannot help you. But you should go to the Buddha. Maybe he can bring your son back to life!"

Kisa Gotami was extremely excited upon hearing the elder's words. She immediately went to the Buddha's residence and pleaded for him to bring her son back to life.

"Kisa Gotami, I have a way to bring your son back to life."

"My Lord, I will do anything to bring my son back"

"If that is the case, then I need you to find me something. Bring me a mustard seed. But it must be taken from a house where no one residing in the house has ever lost a family member. Bring this seed back to me and your son will come back to life."

Having great faith in the Buddha's promise, Kisa Gotami went from house to house, trying to find the mustard seed.

At the first house, a young woman offered to give her some mustard seeds. But when Kisa Gotami asked if she had ever lost a family member to death, the young woman said her grandmother died a few months ago.

Kisa Gotami thanked the young woman and explained why the mustard seeds did not fulfill the Buddha's requirements.

She moved on to the 2nd house. A husband had died a few years ago. The 3rd house had lost an uncle and the 4th house had lost an aunt. She kept moving from house to house, but the answer was all the same—every house had lost a family member to death.

Kisa Gotami finally came to realize that there was no one in the world who had never lost a family member to death. She now understood that death is inevitable and a natural part of life. Putting aside her grief, she buried her son in the forest. She then returned to the Buddha and became his follower.

PRACTICE

When you are ready, consider these reflection questions:

- *What or who do I relate with in this story?*
- *What about my own story resonates with what I'm reading here?*
- *What action or message do I want to take with me?*

When you're ready to close your practice, take a moment to offer up a blessing of Loving Kindness to those you know who are having a difficult time of things. And if it would be helpful, offer this blessing for yourself as well.

> *May you be happy.*
> *May you be healthy.*
> *May you be strong.*
> *May you be at ease.*

DAY 61: THE KINDNESS FACTOR

What to bring to your practice: *Your connection to others, Joy Journal (optional)*

When we spend our time alleviating the suffering of others,
our own suffering tends to lessen as well.

Throughout this week, we've been taking time to consider our interconnectedness and to offer up blessings to those we care about. Today, we are continuing our exploration of Love and Compassion through the lens of kindness. Many believe that our greatest joy occurs when we seek to do good for others—when we not only *wish* them well but when we actually seek to be of service, to offer Loving Kindness.

Consider this story:

Our oldest child had just entered Kindergarten. I was a young mom, relatively new to the city we were living in, and eager to make connections in the community. I found that one easy enough way to do this was to strike up conversations with other parents during drop-offs and pick-ups. On one such day, I learned that it was the birthday of one of the other moms. As I walked back to our home that morning I thought, "I have time. I could make her a cake, and bring it back with me this afternoon."

I can't even remember what kind of a cake it was. But what I do remember was what happened that afternoon. What I thought would be a simple, friendly gesture ended up meaning so much more. To my surprise, the mother started to cry. "You have no idea how much this means to me," she said. "My family lives in Brazil, and I haven't been able to be in touch with them. I miss them so much, and so for you to bring this cake…" The tears flowed. From that moment on, we were invited to all of their family's special occasions.

Now, what isn't shared in that short retelling of my story is that our family was going through a lot as well. We had just transitioned from being a family of three to being a family of 5. One day, we had a 5-year-old, and that was it. The next day, we had a 5-year-old, a 4-year-old, and a 13-month-old. In many ways, our family was in survival mode as we struggled to adjust.

A few years later, we would become a family of 6, adding a newborn baby with only 2 weeks' notice, (and only months after having given away almost all of the baby gear!) It would be then that others would come around us, gathering baby supplies while I rocked a baby in NICU. The day before we brought that baby home, I arrived at the church I was pastoring, bleary-eyed from a night in the hospital, and in came a load of baby stuff, all placed next to the platform where the Christmas tree would go just a couple of months later.

You see, it doesn't matter what we're doing—baking cakes, mowing lawns, holding babies, shoveling snow, fixing a computer, running an errand—the act of being there for someone has a way of unexpectedly raising our levels of joy.

PRACTICE

Having read these words, take a moment to offer yourself a grounding inhale, breathing life into your body and exhaling the weight of any stresses, tensions, and *shoulds* that you might be carrying.

- *Notice if anyone in particular comes to mind, anyone who may be having an experience lately of "coming up short."*

If someone has come to mind, allow yourself to become curious about why that might be and if there are any actions you are feeling motivated to take.

- *If no one in particular comes to mind, consider setting an intention of openness today—to remain willing to be a source of kindness in the world. Perhaps this will look like offering a smile, a compliment, a helping hand...*

Note: If you are setting an intention to return to this practice at a later time today, consider creating a physical reminder for yourself.

And in whatever choices you're making today, before moving on with your day, take a moment to consider those you know who may be in need of a little blessing today, offering these words:

> *May you be happy.*
> *May you be healthy.*
> *May you be strong.*
> *May you be at ease.*

DAY 62: REDUCING SUFFERING, BRINGING JOY

What to bring to your practice: A comfortable space, Joy Journal (optional)

Small actions make big impacts.

As we begin our meditation today, take a moment to offer yourself a couple of life-giving breaths, allowing yourself to be energized by this Source of Life, taking breath deep into the core of your body. And on the exhales, notice how each one releases the weight of the world. Breathing in and breathing out, we set aside our to-do lists, allowing the rest of the day to fade into the background as we arrive here in this present moment.

And then, as we begin to breathe normally, allow your senses to become more fully aware as well. You may take a moment to feel the support of the floor or the chair beneath you, the feel of the air on your skin, the sounds that may be present around you. All of these things we welcome as part of the interconnectedness of our present moment...

...And then, continuing to allow the breath to flow naturally, consider again the words above: *Small actions make big impacts.*

As you hear these words, allow the face of someone you care about —and with whom you have no current conflicts—to come to mind. It may be a family member, a coworker, a neighbor... As their face comes to mind, allow yourself to really see them and imagine that they are seeing you, too.

See the way they style their hair, the way that their eyes smile when they smile at you. Take time to see the depths of their smile. And as you do, offer them a blessing of Loving Kindness:

> *May you be happy.*
> *May you be healthy.*
> *May you be strong.*
> *May you be at ease.*

And now, turn your attention to the face of someone you may be having difficulty with lately. In the same way as before, take the time to really see them. In the interconnectedness of all things, perhaps their eyes offer you a window to their heart or maybe their head. If you can, allow yourself to smile at them from your mind's eye and to see their response to your smile. Consider if it's possible for you to see the interconnectedness between you.

As you sit with this image, if you can, offer them the same blessing of Loving Kindness. If you cannot, offer this blessing towards yourself. But if you can:

> *May you be happy.*
> *May you be healthy.*
> *May you be strong.*
> *May you be at ease.*

Taking time to truly see the people around us can make a tremendous difference in how we interact in the world and experience our lives. As you go about the rest of your day today, try to offer moments of awareness to the world around you and see what arises as you do.

Thank you for joining me today. As you prepare to go into the rest of your day, may these simple acts be a source of joy for you.

DAY 63: SHARING OUR JOY SPARK

What to bring to your practice: *Joy Journal*

Compassion is a contagion worth spreading!

oday we take a moment to celebrate the joy that rises up from within when we take the time to truly see the people around us. Joy, as we have talked about throughout this journey, is the unlimited essence of our being. Every single time we allow ourselves to connect in the world around us, that unlimited essence is given the chance to rise to the front of our awareness. In contrast, when we don't offer ourselves time for this sort of connection, the small self tends to take over. We more easily become irritable, anxious, fearful...

In brief, we stop short of reflecting the preciousness of others back to them. This was a piece of wisdom that I once received in connection to parenting, and it immediately became a spiritual practice for me, not just in parenting but in all of my interactions. To be sure, I have to reset my intention regularly. But whatever else I may be feeling, it is always and forever true that life is precious.

Throughout this week, you've been invited to pray blessings over others. You have been a living, walking, breathing light beam in the world. And that is something worth celebrating!

And so today's spiritual practice: *Sharing our Joy Spark*. As you consider the words above, take some time with the Reflection Prompts below.

PRACTICE

- *What do these words prompt in you? Which of them ring most true to you today?*
- *As you look ahead, how do you want to share your joy spark today? (A smile, a story, a praise, a thanks, a helping hand, a prayer...the possibilities are endless...)*

Today, we celebrate by allowing our compassion to become contagious!

WEEK 10

MEANING & PURPOSE

DAY 64: MINDSETS, ACTIONS, AND CHOICES

What to bring to your practice: *Joy Journal*

What happens is one thing.
How we interpret what happens is another.

As we begin Week 10 of our Joy Journey, first of all, take a moment to offer yourself a centering breath. Way back in Week 1, we started a practice of breathing in life and exhaling out toxicity, of taking Life into the body and releasing tensions and stress on the exhale, because as we read above: There's what *happens*. And then there's how we *interpret* what happens. And so we begin by *choosing* to take a step back, to breathe in and celebrate this moment. And as we intentionally allow the breath to center us in this way, we turn our attention to this 10th week in our Joy Journey, our 10th week of intentionally connecting with Joy, the essence of our being, our 10th week of adding moments of delight to our lives, of returning to that set point over and over again.

PRACTICE

Allowing yourself to breathe normally now, consider this question: *What is "Meaning and Purpose?"*

And in asking the question as a whole, let's actually break the question into two parts, first considering for yourself:

- *What do I derive meaning from in my life?*

I'll give you a moment now to consider the question. If you'd like, feel welcome to jot down a few notes for yourself.

…And now that you've taken even just a moment to begin thinking about where meaning comes from in your life, let's also consider for a moment the question of purpose in our lives. And so, taking in another centering breath, allow yourself time with this question:

- *What is my purpose?*

And again, I'll give you some time to consider the question.

We began our meditation today by asking "What is Meaning and Purpose?" And then, without defining it, we paused to consider what these words mean for us personally. In general, perhaps the easiest way to define meaning and purpose would be to say that meaning and purpose are simply *"what we do and why we do it,"* which means that how we define meaning and purpose for ourselves may well shift from time to time.

This is okay because our reasons for engaging with meaning and purpose in the context of our Joy Journey is to allow more joy into our lives. And the good news is that purpose doesn't have to be accomplished in big things. The significance of such things occurs naturally as we live our lives, as we engage with family, friends, coworkers, members of our community…

Engaging our meaning and purpose is a way to focus our energies, find grounding, and experience connection. In a world of possibility, meaning and purpose help us understand our what and our why.

The question is: *How do we begin to understand our own sense of meaning & purpose?*

There are probably many ways we could go about trying to answer that question. But for today, and for much of this week, we're going to use the act of storytelling to aid us in our exploration.

And so today, we begin by using an ancient discernment practice developed by St. Ignatius of Loyola. We begin by naming for ourselves: *What is bringing us life and what is taking life from us?*

And so, either in thinking about your day yesterday or the day you just had, consider one of the following pairs of questions:

- *What has helped me find joy today?*
- *What has not helped me find joy today?*

- *When have I felt most alive today?*
- *When have I felt life draining from me today?*

- *When have I felt most connected today?*
- *When have I felt least connected today?*

Using whichever set of questions you most relate to, take a couple of moments now to consider what comes to mind.

Throughout this week, we'll continue to tell our story as a means of increasing our quality of life where joy is concerned. As we do, continue naming and then sitting with your responses, looking for patterns that might emerge that will help you find even more grounding, focus, and connection in your life.

But for now, allow yourself to take one more life-giving inhale, allowing it to move deep into the core of your being, and then allowing the breath to release again, sending life out into the world as you go. Thank you for your practice today. May you be well as you go about the rest of your day.

DAY 65: THE SIMPLE JOYS

What to bring to your practice: *Joy Journal*

We feel most alive when we have found something to live for.

As we continue contemplating meaning and purpose in our lives this week, once again, we emphasize the idea that meaning and purpose don't have to be complex. Certainly, it's fair to also say that there may be moments in our lives when we realize it's time for a dramatic shift. But that being said, it's very likely the case that, on most days, meaning and purpose are as simple as naming those things that bring us joy. And then, once we have named those things, intentionally sprinkling our lives with them as often as we can.

PRACTICE

- *Naming 5 things that make you happy*

To say a bit more about this, in my own life, there are certain things that make me really happy, things like artwork, sunshine in my work spaces, and pictures of people I love. And since I know this about myself, I have sprinkled these things into my world.

Other sorts of things on my list, however, like clean bathrooms and empty laundry baskets, are there for a different sort of reason. They point to a certain sort of anxiety that can creep in and bog me down, making me feel less settled in my life. And even in this, because I know this about myself, I can create systems to stay on top of some of it so that my happiness quotient isn't dragged down by these seem-ingly little things.

A bonus thing that makes me very happy: Leaving space on Saturday mornings to go more slowly. This one is really about giving myself the gift of time, knowing that every other day tends to be scheduled.

And so that's a little bit about me. Now it's your turn. Grab your Joy Journal and consider today's Reflection Prompt:

- *Name 5 things that make you happy.*

As we close today, may your day be filled with many somethings to live for, and may they allow you to feel truly alive.

DAY 66: TO BE AS WATER

What to bring to your practice: *Water, Joy Journal*

SEARCHING FOR OCEAN
A reactive mind
Takes the shape of a droplet
Searching for ocean
—August 2022

In the Tao te Ching, we are offered the invitation to flow like water. Lao Tzu tells us that the fluidity of water is powerful enough to wear away the rigidity of rock, and in this fluidness, water becomes even more powerful than rock. When we apply these ideas to ourselves, allowing ourselves to become more fluid and to flow like water, it can allow us to adopt flexible mindsets, to grow, and to change.

The struggle exists in the need for practice. The ego is constantly

returning, not to childlike awe and wonder, but to childlike preoccu-
pation with self. Though we appear separate from one another, we
are, in fact, a part of the very same ocean.

PRACTICE

And so today's spiritual practice is to *spend time with water*. This could
be rain falling from the sky, a glass of water, a shower, a stream, a
beach…any water you can be with. As you do, you may wish to keep
your Joy Journal nearby.

- *What is the water speaking to me about?*

When your practice is complete, return to the set of questions
found below and originally asked on Day 64. With our attention
turned towards joy in the context of meaning and purpose, allow the
water to inspire your noticing and naming, choosing at least one pair
from the three sets of questions below.

- *What has helped me find joy today?*
- *What has not helped me find joy today?*

- *When have I felt most alive today?*
- *When have I felt life draining from me today?*

- *When have I felt most connected today?*
- *When have I felt least connected today?*

DAY 67: FACING FEAR

What to bring to your practice: *Joy Journal*

Joy is not dependent on outcomes.

*a*t the beginning of this week, we defined meaning and purpose simply as *"what we do and why we do it."* On the other side of that, there is the "what we are not doing and why we are not doing it." For example, perhaps I choose not to stay up too late because I'm not my best self in the morning if I'm feeling too tired. This is a great reason not to do something!

However, what about when we're not doing something because those somethings are connected to difficulties we feel unsure about. When this is the case, we may find that life begins to feel a lot less joyful. And so to help us consider what this might mean for us personally:

PRACTICE

- *Do not be afraid of being afraid*

We'll begin with a story:

One day, one of our kids was feeling super afraid because it was time for a vaccination. And let me just tell you, there was a lot of emotional energy pumping! So many tears were flowing, and the nurses were doing their usual, "Mom, can you make sure to put your arms around her real tight?" (I'll let you in on a little secret: I don't like shots either, so assume that I'm having my own internal struggle even as I try to model bravery.)

But as vaccinations tend to go, a couple of seconds later, it was all over. And to the surprise of my little one, she hadn't even felt the poke. In complete shock, she stopped crying and exclaimed, "That was it?!"

"That was it," the nurse echoed.

Still feeling surprised at how easy the whole ordeal had been, our child started to laugh as her sense of dread began to shift to something more akin to relief. And as she did, the nurse said, "Remember this moment the next time you come."

And in so many ways, isn't this just how life goes sometimes? We're waiting and waiting with all of this fear and expectation for what is yet to come, only to find that when we arrive at that much-anticipated-much-dreaded moment, it's not nearly as horrible as we had been anticipating. But how easy it is to get on that mental treadmill, imagining all of those worst-case scenarios only to find that none of that is what actually ends up happening.

Now, emotionally speaking, our fears are our fears. And as we've said many times on this journey now, acknowledging how we feel is an important part of our lived experience, because if we are trying to repress any one emotion, we're going to inadvertently repress them all. That being the case, we are very much helped by learning to say to ourselves, "I feel afraid, and that is normal. I feel anxious, and that is to be expected."

The human body has these emotional connections, and that is okay. We just don't want our emotions to stop us from living our lives. And so sometimes, where our joy is concerned, we're going to have to embrace that we have these fears. And then, we're going to want to offer ourselves a lot of compassion and mercy. This really is difficult.

Do acknowledge that you are afraid. But don't let it stop you from following your path towards meaning and purpose.

As you read these words, consider the Reflection Prompts below:

- *Is there anything holding me back lately?*

- *Is there something I'm afraid of, or upset about lately, that is keeping me from experiencing Joy as the unlimited essence of my being?*

- *Are there any (creative) steps I could take that would help me respond to the opportunity that life is offering me at this moment?*

As you close your practice today, consider closing with this breath prayer:

Inhale: *Inhaling Peace and Light*
Exhale: *Exhaling Joy and Love*

DAY 68: WHEN ORDINARY IS DIVINE

What to bring to your practice: *Joy Journal*

Ordinary isn't really a thing. It's all extraordinary.

As we continue our contemplation of purpose and meaning, we turn our attention to the things in our day that may seem incredibly ordinary. It's always tempting to hope that revelation will come in big, grandiose ways that will be impossible to miss. But more often than not, the Divine speaks to us in the context of our simple, everyday lives. In the end, this makes a lot of sense. It's personal. It connects our physical world with the spiritual world. And at times it allows us to have a full-body, sensory experience.

PRACTICE

Consider the words below using the prompts that follow:

LIVING WITH MESS

You can't journey out
Until you can live with mess,
Until you can see the beauty in that, too.
The mess belongs. It must belong.

You can't sterilize the mess.
It has to stay.
And it doesn't mean you can't find peace
It just means the mess is part of it.

Floating bubble, soft and round
Colorful with miracle
Floating without sound

Iridescent beauty
Gleaming, glittering, glory

Refuge in the middle of mess.

You can live with mess.
—April 2023

AFTER THE 1ST READING

- *What parts of this reflection are catching your attention today?*

AFTER THE 2ND READING

- *Why do you suppose this is what's standing out to you?*

AFTER THE 3RD READING

- *What do these words inspire you towards?*

AFTER THE 4TH READING

- *What aspects of your day bring meaning and purpose to your life?*

DAY 69: WALKING THE WALK

What to bring to your practice: *Space to walk, Joy Journal*

A good walk is sometimes all that's really needed.

*A*s we've talked about this week, discerning meaning and purpose can sometimes feel like too big a thing. How am I going to find—*and do!*— my one unique purpose?! It's a lot of pressure. And what's more, the concept of one unique purpose can begin to make us feel as though there's only one *obvious* path for us in life.

And so as we continue to pursue meaning and purpose as part of raising our qualitative experience of life:

PRACTICE

• *Walking*

There's a labyrinth at Glastonbury Abbey in Hingham, Mass-achusetts. It's set back a bit on the property, past the parking lot, past the buildings, past the statues and the gardens, tucked away between a circle of trees. At the mouth of the labyrinth is a little sign that says, "It is solved by walking," a quote from St. Augustine.

The act of walking can have a multitude of positive effects on our bodies. As our limbs begin to move, we may find that, in the same way muscles can move towards relaxation and loosening, so too does our creative energy start to flow and our perspective begin to widen when we engage in the act of movement.

And so, once again, you'll find the reflection prompts below that we used on Days 64 and 66. If you are able to get outside to walk, you're welcome to do so. But walking meditations can also be done in a space the size of a single room so long as you don't try to walk too quickly.

Wherever you choose to walk, begin by offering yourself a centering practice, whether that be taking time to focus on your breath or using your senses to become aware of your surroundings. These centering moments give you space to be fully present to the gift of this moment now.

Once you have taken a moment or two with your opening prac-tice, use one of the pairs of questions from the possible prompts below. And as you walk, rather than trying to actively "accomplish" the questions, allow the responses to come as they come. In this case, we aren't trying to solve it with our minds. We're allowing—and trusting—movement to work its wonders.

When your walk is complete, consider jotting down whatever came to mind in your Joy Journal.

- *What has helped me find joy today?*
- *What has not helped me find joy today?*

- *When have I felt most alive today?*
- *When have I felt life draining from me today?*

- *When have I felt most connected today?*
- *When have I felt least connected today?*

DAY 70: CELEBRATING YOUR STORY

What to bring to your practice: *Joy Song, a comfortable space*
Optional: Movement, Joy Journal

There will always be twists and turns in the story.
Even so, enjoy the bright spots.

*I*t's celebration day!! Throughout this week, we've taken time to consider questions of meaning and purpose that will surely be asked again as we journey forward.

But for today, we celebrate because celebration is an important part of our overall well-being. Celebration is a stress-reliever, a mood-lifter, and an energy booster.

PRACTICE

- *Celebration*

To help you, it's time to return to your Joy Song—or any other song that sparks celebration in you.

First, allow yourself to take in the song, noticing any ways in which your body wants to join in, whether it's a smile and a bop of the head or a full-body, arms-in-the-air sort of thing. Either way, this is your moment to celebrate those resilient gifts that reside within you, those things that you love to do, that bring you energy, that make you feel alive to the point that hours seem to fly by.

When you are ready, close your practice with this question:

- *What am I taking with me from this week of exploration?*

WEEK 11

ACCEPTANCE & HARMONY

DAY 71: LIMITING BELIEFS

What to bring to your practice: *Joy Journal*

Set a goal to make joy a part of your days.

*H*ello dear Joy Journeyer! Welcome to week 11— Acceptance & Harmony. Acceptance can be thought of as the act of engaging life on its own terms rather than continually feeling as though life is not as we want it to be, which can lead to living in a perpetual state of reaction.

And, as we'll be talking about this week, living in, and creating harmony, is an integral part of that journey. We need some amount of order in our lives to accept the chaos. We need a way to make sense of our lives, to be able to discern what is truly in need of change and what is actually the result of our sometimes overactive and reactionary minds. In short, living in harmony where we can is key to practicing acceptance.

204 | KRISTINA STONE KAISER

And so to begin, a bit of good news: All of us possess the ability to accept things as they are, and it can be helpful to celebrate the instances where this is true. Maybe we scratch the car, burn dinner, oversleep, get sick, break a glass, have rain on the day of our party... and we actually accept it. Perhaps we take one of those life-giving breaths, and we then face reality, clean up the mess, pivot the plans, and on and on. For every single moment that we do this successfully, that is worth celebrating. Go you!

That being said, acceptance is notoriously difficult for most of us. When things aren't going according to how we would have hoped, it's often the case that something inside us rejects this alternative reality quite profoundly. The childlike us, rather than wondering what great, new adventure could be next, goes, "No, no, no, no, no, no, no, no, no, no...no, no, no, no, no, no, no...no, no, no. No. NO!"

PRACTICE

And so today, we're going to journey towards joy by working through our limiting beliefs—a state of mind or belief that restricts you in some way, thoughts that make you feel *less-than*.

The struggle here is that most of us are so comfortable with our limiting beliefs that we don't even recognize them for what they are. So to help you, below you'll find a short list of limiting beliefs that can serve to get you started, and as always, feel free to think beyond the list as well.

12 EXAMPLES OF LIMITING BELIEFS

1. I'm just not as good/talented as others.
2. I can't be trusted with —.
3. I'm no good at —.
4. Everyone else has all the luck/ability.
5. Everyone else in my family is —.
6. I never win.

7. There isn't enough to go around.
8. I'm no good at managing —.
9. I can't control myself with —.
10. I'm just not as — as some people.
11. — is just something I have to live with.
12. People won't like me if I —.

Once you've identified something you believe to be a limiting belief in your life, using your Joy Journal, ask yourself:

- *What additional negative thinking tends to come from this limiting belief?*
- *In what ways are these beliefs proving unhelpful for me?*
- *What life-giving truth could I offer myself should these limiting beliefs return?*

Before we go any further, we need to have another mini celebration. Identifying limiting beliefs is a powerful, life-changing act. Somewhere there are balloons and bubbles floating around in your honor. Congratulations!

As you prepare to go about the rest of your day, practice repeating your life-giving truth a couple of times. You may even wish to post it somewhere so that you can revisit it often.

DAY 72: THIS TOO BELONGS

What to bring to your practice: *A comfortable space*

Life becomes more joyful when we can accept our circumstances.

$\mathcal{Y}$esterday we began exploring the fact that most of us have a sense of how we'd like things to be. And yet, much of the time, we may not even be aware that we're living our lives with a list of ideals that we would like to see play out the way we see them in our heads. We want people to act the way we want them to, traffic and lines at the store to flow in our favor, people to recognize us for our hard work, our bodies to cooperate with even our most remote efforts to be healthy. If we garden, ideally, it would rain at least every couple of days. If we want to build something, ideally, the cost of wood would be at an all-time low. And on and on.

The ability to be present in each moment is about accepting the vulnerability, discomfort, and anxiety of everyday life. As we sit with this idea of acceptance, while we aren't talking about ignoring reality, we are talking about dealing with life as it is and journeying ahead from the place we actually are.

- This is what is at this very moment.
- This is reality right now.

We can certainly name what is difficult about that. We can admit that we don't like it. We can make a plan to bring harmony back into our lives. But it will do us no good to simply be upset that life isn't as we wish it to be.

Joy comes when we are able to accept our lives as they are. And so today, our spiritual practice is a breath prayer using the words, *"This too belongs."*

Breath Prayer
Inhale: *This too*
Exhale: *Belongs*

To begin, offer yourself a couple of life-giving inhales and tension-releasing exhales. Take a moment to allow the eyes and the corners of the mouth to soften. Become aware of the things surrounding you right now that are pleasant and bring you a sense of comfort and gratitude. Even in the midst of difficulty—and there are always difficulties—there are also good things. We are alive, and that is a little bit of celebration all on its own.

When you are ready, allow your attention to turn to something you wish were different– a circumstance, the timing of something, a situation—something that feels as though it is taking away from joy in your life. If you wish, allow your hands to cover your heart, offering yourself a bit of Loving Kindness. This part of life feels difficult, and it's okay to acknowledge that, even as we're working to accept our circumstance as it is.

As you sit calmly in this space, begin your breath prayer, repeating it numerous times, even for up to 5 minutes if you can, allowing space for deeper waves of peace to come the longer you practice.

Inhale: *This too*
Exhale: *Belongs*

...Perhaps close your practice with a couple of "Living Ahs," inhaling deeply and then letting out an "Ahhhhhh" as you exhale. Return to this practice whenever you feel it is needed.

DAY 73: DISCOVERING HARMONY IN NATURE

What to bring to your practice: *Your natural environment*
Optional: Joy Journal, a camera

To look into nature is to gain understanding.

id you know that much of nature grows in a spiral pattern? This was discovered by a 13th-century mathematician, Leonardo of Pisa, also known as Fibonacci, and you can often observe this pattern easily in flowers. But a quick trip out to the garden reveals a similar story, which can be seen in the following photos.

Romaine.

Baby Bok Choy.

Red Leaf Lettuce.

Kohlrabi. All photos July 2023.

Throughout this week, we're talking about Acceptance and Harmony. Our environment is full of complexity. A plant, in many ways, seems to miraculously grow. But plant systems can easily be foiled—fungus, not enough nutrients in the soil, not enough water, too much water, not enough sun, too much sun, predators—too many, not enough…

The world is full of complexity. But in the midst of that complexity, there's also harmony, things that bring about a sense of order, a sense of ease. And so our spiritual practice for today is *discovering harmonies in nature.*

PRACTICE

You may wish to grab your Joy Journal or your camera for this one. And if you can, this would be a great day to take your practice outside. But if it's not possible, perhaps plants in your home or even the photos above will do.

Acceptance and Harmony are ways of accessing Joy, the unlimited essence of our being. Our natural world experiences much difficulty. In the Northern Midwest, harsh thunderstorms, ice storms, hail, and snow all contribute to the struggle of everyday life for living things. Some trees tell the story, leaning slightly to one side, finding a way to live with one less branch than they had last year, and so on.

But through it all, they look for a way to thrive in spite of it all, including by growing in spiral patterns, which often allows for the greatest number of seeds, petals, or leaves to grow. So today we turn our attention to living things, looking deeper into nature to gain understanding.

Take some time to observe how an experience of thriving or overcoming in the natural world is happening around you. If you want, take your own pictures, create what you see on the page, or journal your musings. And when you are ready, ask yourself:

- *What is nature teaching me today about Acceptance and Harmony?*

DAY 74: CHOOSING ACCEPTANCE

What to bring to your practice: *Joy Journal*

Rather than demanding that life meet our conditions,
we can, instead, tune our hearts, minds, and bodies towards joy.

*M*any things in our lives have a story to tell. Metals lose their shine. Bowls become chipped. Windowsills become spotted with rain and filled with deposits of dust. In the same way, evidence lives in us that we, too, have traveled a few miles, weathered a few storms, seen our expectations dashed.

As we read above, we may well have tried demanding that life meet us on our own terms. But as we've been talking about this week, Joy is an experience we can have even when things do not turn out as we first imagined them to be. To accept our lives as they are is a simple but effective path towards Joy.

PRACTICE

And so today, we draw our inspiration from the reflection below titled "All of this Belongs." Take a few moments to read the reflection, reading slowly several times, maybe even at least one of those times out loud. When you are ready, proceed to the Reflection Prompt that follows.

ALL OF THIS BELONGS

There are no clean circles,
No perfect boundaries.
It's blended everything.
Blended families
Blended lives
Blended stories
Blended faiths

On ramps
Off ramps
Coming and going

All of this belongs

Malady and wellness
Happiness and sadness
Triumph and defeat
Gah! So much defeat!

There, there.
All of this belongs.

Jagged lines and smooth
Soft blankets and hard stones

Bees sting and ants bite
But breezes blow and waters flow

It's all there.
And all of this belongs.
—April 2023

REFLECT

- *Today, instead of being in reaction about — for not being —, I choose —.*

Allow this to be a statement that you live with as you go about your day, returning to it whenever you feel the need.

DAY 75: HARMONIES HELP

What to bring to your practice: *Joy Song, Joy Journal*

Joy is within our grasp, if only we will tune in to it.

As we continue our exploration of Acceptance and Harmony this week, we turn our attention to music. Music offers us both harmonies and dissonances. For anyone who has listened to an extremely dissonant piece…or perhaps played the 2 notes simultaneously on the keyboard that were right next to each other…you will know that the ear eventually tires of this experience. Something in us intuitively looks for—longs for—resolution. In fact, if a musician plays a series of chords for us, ending on what we would call an unresolved chord, we will instinctually finish the piece in our heads. Many of us, and particularly those of us with a Western-trained ear, are hard-wired to look for resolution after dissonance.

Furthermore, we also know that music, particularly when experienced with others, is known to create a sense of unity at the physio-logical level. Joining in with others in a musical way, whether that be a choir, a band, a concert, or a bucket-drum circle, gives us a sense of feeling unified, connected...happy...joyful. The technical term for this is "synchrony." As we learned from our week on Love and Compassion, part of the joy we get from the experience of synchrony occurs as our focus very naturally begins to shift from our own needs to the needs of the group.

PRACTICE

For today, our spiritual practice involves cueing up our Joy Songs, allowing the music to draw us in, and encouraging our internal harmonies to swell. As you hear your song, purpose yourself to be fully present to the sounds, the way one note becomes more, the way the sounds intermingle with one another, the rises and the falls of the music, how the line becomes increasingly complex while the familiar continues to anchor everything together. When your listening is complete, spend some time with the Reflection Prompts below.

- *What familiar thing(s) anchor(s) my life and allow(s) for the unexpected and the complexities of life to belong?*

- *Are there other anchors I would like to add to my life, anchors that would add more harmony so that I have space and time to ever increasingly recognize the joys in my life?*

DAY 76: CREATING HARMONY

What to bring to your practice: *A mess*
Optional: A camera, Joy Journal

The secret to joyfully beginning again is accepting that nothing remains as it was.

Oftentimes, we may identify joy with a sense of feeling delighted in being free. We may conjure up images of children gleefully turning in circles. We may imagine celebrations, of New Year's Eves becoming New Year's Days while people shout, "Happy New Year!" We may imagine moments on the beach, wind blowing through our hair while waves lap happily against the shore. Moments of freedom!

These are great experiences, each one of them a gift in their own way. And! There is this other quite surprising way in which we might experience joy: The beauty of order.

Did you know that order can be delightful?

If this seems surprising to you, think about how you feel after organizing a closet, desk, or bookshelf, that little satisfied feeling you get from those little vacuum lines in the carpet, or even how you feel when you walk by a picture hanging crooked on the wall...and you just...boop...straighten that edge right quick.

It turns out, our brains are hardwired to see symmetry, to live in the context of an environment that makes us feel stable, balanced, and grounded. In fact, research shows that when our environments offer us a certain amount of order (felt safety), it frees us to take a few risks.

PRACTICE

And so today, we engage the spiritual practice of *creating order*!

That's right, our practice today is to spend a few moments organizing something. Maybe you've been meaning to put your books in color order, alphabetical order, size order...Maybe there's a stack of mail you've been meaning to tackle. Maybe it's as simple as taking a moment to make your bed.

Whatever it is, as you spend those few moments bringing order to your life, pay attention to that little bit of delight that begins to emerge. Maybe even celebrate it by taking a picture of your work. Allow yourself to feel an inordinate amount of pleasure by creating harmony in your physical environment.

Go ahead, take pure joy in beginning again.

DAY 77: LOOK AROUND

What to bring to your practice: *Your surroundings*
Optional: Joy Journal, camera, etc.

*Joy comes as we are able to see something of the Divine
everywhere and in everything.*

Congratulations!! You have spent an entire week offering
yourself the chance to cultivate more joy in your life through
the practices of Acceptance and Harmony. Three cheers for you!

Today we are invited to consider the possibility of seeing the
Divine in all things. To help us with this, we're told that Joy—the
unlimited essence of our being—rises up within when we begin to see
the world around us as one integrated whole. When this happens, our
lives become harmonious. We stop trying to separate Divine Presence
from the Ordinary.

PRACTICE

And so today's spiritual practice: *Look around!*

- *Where do you see Divine Presence today—maybe even for the first time?*

You may wish to put your answers in your Joy Journal. Or, if you prefer, take a picture. Maybe even share your experience with someone else. Three cheers for you and three cheers for beholding the Divine in all things!

WEEK 12

SURPRISE & WONDER

DAY 78: ABOUNDING JOYFUL SURPRISES

What to bring to your practice: *Your environment*
Optional: Joy Journal and/or camera

~

A SMILE
I hear your story
I watch as your eyes light up
A smile fills the soul
—August 2022

*W*elcome to the 12th week of your Joy Journey! As we begin our 2nd to last week together (!), we turn our attention to the theme of surprise and wonder.

To begin our exploration, perhaps consider a time when you were simply going about your day. Maybe your brow was furrowed a little as you walked along, deeply engaged with your inner world. And then, as if out of nowhere, someone broke into your little bubble, perhaps with a cheery hello, stopping to tell you your shoelace was untied, or maybe even offering you a compliment. Whatever their way in, instantly you felt your face shift. You smiled and you connected with that other person, if only for a brief moment. And amazingly, after you had each gone your separate ways, the smile didn't immediately fade back into deep introspection. It took a moment as the effect of your interaction lingered and became integrated into your being.

These sorts of moments happen with some amount of regularity in our lives. At times, you may even be the one doing the breaking in, starting up a brief conversation at the grocery store or offering your own friendly hello as you walk down the street.

Or, to shift gears for a moment, ever been on an airplane and opened a water bottle with a straw-type design? If so, you may well have gotten a little wet thanks to these things we like to call "pressure buildup" and "changing altitudes."

When these surprising sorts of things happen, it's only natural that we're shocked at first. Eyes go wide, mouth gapes open, head starts to shuffle one side to the next...but then we gradually begin to realize what has happened. And as we do, the face usually softens and, as the shock of the moment wears off, we begin to laugh because, oh my goodness, can you believe what just happened to us?! That was surprising!

These moments, as we said, are really just that—a quick moment in time. But, it turns out that the effect of wonder and surprise are quite a bit more far-reaching than the moment itself. And when we are able to take those moments in—continuing to practice the awareness we began cultivating at the beginning of our Joy Journey—those moments can bring about an upward spiral of joy and joy-related emotions. What's more, those moments have the potential to increase our sense of overall well-being, offering us the invitation for even more curiosity and connection.

In a nutshell, we begin to experience a life that is lit up and cluttered with joy, a world where our soul is filled with smiling.

PRACTICE

In our usual way, we practice centering and grounding by becoming still, taking in that life-giving breath and exhaling away all the toxicity that's been building up in your body. As you begin to feel connected to this moment now, start to *look slowly around the space you are in.* Chances are, you're somewhat familiar with your surroundings, which means that much of what's around you is being filtered out by your brain. But now that you are looking with more of yourself:

- *What do you see that brings you joy, maybe even surprises you?*
- *Does what you're seeing bring you delight or help you to feel connected?*

Take special note of whatever comes to mind, perhaps jotting a few notes down in your Joy Journal or taking a picture or two.

Note: Throughout this week, each day's practice will close with a "For the Day" section. These prompts are designed to help you find and receive the benefits of the actual experiences of surprise and wonder in your day-to-day life. To what may come!

FOR THE DAY

- *Keep a running list of things that surprise you, cause you to laugh, and just generally "fill your soul with a smile."*

DAY 79: LIGHTENING THE MOOD

What to bring to your practice: *Joy Journal*

Life becomes more joyful when it can include the unexpected.

As we continue exploring this week's theme of surprise and wonder, we hone in on the great human experience of being surprised by one another and we revisit the power of laughter. Laughter is a common response to surprise. It acts as a welcome release in the midst of tense moments and serves as a medicinal elixir in difficult conversations. It's the salve we turn to when we find ourselves in unfamiliar territory.

But whether we're talking about taking a moment to laugh, getting a drink of water, or going for a walk, what we're ultimately talking about is lightening the mood. We're talking about reengaging with our sense of Joy so that we can begin to think more fluidly, accept differences, find potential in possibility, and, ultimately, let go of the rigidity that tends to come when we're feeling threatened or unsafe.

PRACTICE

And so today, our spiritual practice involves *allowing the surprising to lighten the mood.*

Consider the story below (or, perhaps, a story from your own life) and then respond to the reflection prompt that follows. When your practice feels complete, take note of your "for the day" practice and keep the fun going.

FROM THE MOUTH OF BABES

When one of our kids was in about 1st grade, we were talking about... something meaningful, I'm sure...when our 1st grader, in their sweetest voice said of their father and I, "You're not people..."

Pause with me here in this feeling. Woe to the one who has endured the hormonal ups and downs of pregnancy, the sleepless nights, the desire to comfort a pained child, only to hear that child say without hesitation, "You're not people..."

...but wait for it...there's more...

"...You're family."

Immediately we burst out laughing, and our hearts became a mushy pile of goo for this amazingly insightful child who had so innocently destroyed us only to immediately lift us up higher than we thought possible. Over a decade later, that moment continues to incite laughter and a lightening of the mood for our entire family: *"You're not people...(long dramatic pause)...you're family!"*

And now it's your turn.

- *In considering any or all aspects of well-being that might apply—physical, emotional, mental, spiritual—use your Joy Journal to take note of how you feel after spending some time with something unexpected that turns out to be quite wonderful.*

FOR THE DAY

- *Continue keeping a running list today of the things that surprise you, cause you to laugh, "fill your soul with a smile," and/or help you connect with others on a human level.*

DAY 80: WONDERS ALL AROUND

What to bring to your practice: *Your natural environment, Joy Journal (optional)*

~

FOUND IN THE TRANTRA SHASTRAS
From Joy springs all creation
By Joy it is sustained
Toward Joy it proceeds
And to Joy it returns
–Translation by Amit Mookerjee

Our exploration of surprise and wonder expands today to the subject of our natural world. The text above tells us creation is born of Joy and that Joy sustains that very same creation. In response, creation intuitively begins to move towards Joy, as if the experience of being alive requires creation to journey back into the arms of Joy again.

What an amazing idea! And in fact, where joy is concerned, our world turns out to be quite full of energy, surprises, and wonders. There are the visible effects of static electricity—hilarious when it's someone else's hair sticking to the wall. The delight of rainbows reflecting on walls, the awe of waves as they lap against the shore, and the mesmerizing experience of getting to see a shooting star.

Our world is constantly expressing itself, enthusiastically responding to wind, blooming with delight, sparkling in the sun, all of it reminding us that Joy is all around, if only we will open ourselves to the wonder of it.

PRACTICE

Below are two pictures of the exact same tree, one taken in the early days of spring and the other taken in the deep months of winter. Take a moment or two to sit with these images, allowing your eye to be drawn to whatever catches your attention, noticing any reactions that come up for you. When you are ready, continue to the Reflection Prompts below.

- *What wonders arise in me as I take these two images in?*
- *How do each of these pictures depict Joy as described above in the Tantra Shastras?*

FOR THE DAY

- *Practice looking around today for those "unseen" energies—sun rays through the clouds, the movement of curtains...What are you coming in contact with that allows you to experience wonder?*

DAY 81: LIGHTENING THE LOAD

What to bring to your practice: *Your community, Joy Journal*

*We need human connection in the same way
we need food, water, and exercise.*

*E*arlier this week, we talked about how the power of surprise and wonder in our interactions can widen our perspective, lessening rigidity in our mindsets, and relieving feelings of tension and anxiety. At other times, the surprise of finding another by our side has yet another effect—that of lightening the load. No longer do we feel as if we are carrying the burden alone. Instead, because we are seen, because we are supported—maybe even especially when we weren't expecting it—we find that something rises up within and we are able to carry on, to move forward, to survive the moment we are living, and then the next, and then the next.

PRACTICE

Today's spiritual practice is about identifying those people in our lives that make up our circle of support. Certainly, others may unexpectedly surprise us with their care at just the right moment. But it's also helpful to spend time naming—and even having conversations with—those who play those meaningful roles in our lives on a regular basis. Spend some time with the story below and then respond to the Reflection Prompt that follows. When your practice is complete, make a note of your "For the Day" practice to aid your ongoing experience of connection.

DEREK REDMOND AND THE 1992 BARCELONA SUMMER OLYMPICS

The year is 1992 and the Summer Olympics are happening in Barcelona. The event is the Men's 400-meter dash, and it's the semifinals. The runner is Derek Redmond who holds the British record in the sport and is favored to win.

The gun goes off. The racers jump from their blocks and begin their incredible sprint—one full lap around the track. But just over halfway through the race, the unthinkable happens. There is a searing pain in Redmond's hamstring, and he instinctively reaches for the back of his leg, falling to the ground.

Immediately the media begins to close in, cameras and microphones all pointed at Derek while the rest of the runners in his heat, as if in the blink of an eye, cross the finish line. The race is over. But what's this? Redmond stands up and begins to limp towards the finish line, 250 meters yet to go.

Officials try to stop him, but he continues, meanwhile, another man is pushing past security guards as they try to hold him back. The man is shouting, "That's my son!" As the security guards relent, Jim Redmond, comes alongside his limping son, puts one arm around his shoulders and as they continue together, Jim tells Derek, *"You don't have to do this."*

But Derek, through tears, tells his father, *"Yes, I do."*

His father's reply to him: *"Then we're going to finish this together."*

Giving in to not having to bear the weight of this unexpected burden alone, Derek turns into his father, crying on his shoulder as they move forward together. Through the pain and the struggle, they continue their race with 65,000 people now on their feet, each one of those onlookers cheering them on through every painful step of the way.

…As we look back on that moment, we reflect on the courage it took for Redmond to stand up again and keep going. And even more importantly, we remember that when he came to the end of himself, he was met by the support of his father. What he could not bear alone, they bore together. And in doing so, despite the numerous discomforts they faced, they were able to keep going. It started with an act of courage. It continued by way of love and support that helped to lighten the load.

PRACTICE

- *Make a list of people you rely on, naming what it is you rely on them for.*
- *Do they know they play this role?*
- *Are there others you would like to invite into your circle of support?*

FOR THE DAY

- *Take time to pay attention today. Does someone do something that surprises you in a good way, leading you to feel less anxious, more connected, or more joyous?*

DAY 82: THIS MAGICAL LIFE

What to bring to your practice: *Joy Journal*

Life is magical and magic is everywhere.

We humans, whether we know it or not, live by various sets of laws and expectations, things that make the world feel safe enough. We expect that if we drop something off the counter, it will fall to the ground. We expect the sun to rise in the east and set in the west. We expect that people treat each other with a certain amount of dignity and respect. These and many more are the laws and expectations we live by. But it is also the case that we encounter things we neither expect nor have an explanation for.

In order to "resolve" these issues, at times, our curiosity will cause us to go looking for an answer, to pursue, to explore. At other times, we might simply choose to stand in awe, allowing the wonder and surprise to wash over us. There are those moments where we choose to live with the mystery, enjoying it and marveling in it because life feels balanced enough, ordered enough. And those are the moments we can simply allow ourselves to be delighted, leading us to be more fluid, accepting things as they are, thinking outside the box, and so on.

PRACTICE

Today's spiritual practice involves spending some time with your Joy Journals using the reflection prompt below.

- *Consider a time when you were pleasantly surprised, delighted, or left in awe. Place yourself in the moment, remembering as many details as you can. As you revisit this memory, what does it cause you to wonder about?*

FOR THE DAY

- *Take time to be present to wonder today. Even if they are small, actively share your stories of wonder and surprise with others.*

DAY 83: WONDER-FUL MOVEMENT

What to bring to your practice: *The World, Joy Journal (optional)*

Joy impacts us because we forget it's possible.

This week we've spent a lot of time considering experiences because, as we read above, joy is found in the context of experience. This week has been all about the journey, about connecting to what's possible. Throughout these 90 days, our goal has been to do this in as many ways as we can, to explore the depths—the nooks and crannies of where Joy exists in our lives.

And when it comes to describing Joy, wonder is just one of any number of words we might use to try and describe this unlimited essence within. We are amazed by it, awed, surprised, shocked, speechless…It's not quite familiar, slightly different from what we'd normally expect.

One way to experience this wonder is to travel, which may well be an excellent spiritual practice. But for the purposes of our Joy Journey together, it just isn't practical to invite you to get on a train, a plane, or a boat yet today. But! We *can* transport ourselves to another time and place using our imaginations.

PRACTICE

Today's practice involves integrating movement into our memories. Begin by offering yourself a life-centering breath, arriving fully into the present moment and allowing all that is yet to come fall away for a moment. Take as many of these breaths as you need to feel centered, grounded, and connected.

Once your body is calm, allow yourself to remember a special place in your life—*a place that delights you*. As this place comes to mind, begin to look around and notice:

- *What movement can you see?*
- *What movement exists in you?*
- *Can you embody any of that movement or offer yourself movement in the context of your memory?*
- *What moves in you as you observe this place? If there is movement of your own you'd like to explore, consider making it a part of your "for the day" reflections.*

FOR THE DAY

- *Actively seek out wonder in your journey today as you move about your day. Notice how it impacts you.*

DAY 84: CELEBRATING WEIRDLY WONDERFUL

What to bring to your practice: *Joy Journal*

~

A recipe for increasing Joy: Add a little spice.

*H*ave you ever considered that weird can be wonderful?

The word "weird" is often attributed to things that make us feel uncomfortable, for experiences that are less familiar to us. Quite often, when someone says something is "weird," they tend to mean that they don't know if they like it.

But as you might guess, today we are reclaiming the word "weird" and attributing it to things that bring delight. On this final day of contemplating surprise and wonder, you are invited to celebrate that which is "weirdly wonderful."

The little ways in which we experience surprise and wonder every single day are the spice of life. They are the fun that make the unbearable more bearable.

PRACTICE

Today's spiritual practice involves *inviting a little wackiness* into your day. Start from the vantage point of your surroundings?

What can you see around you that might be considered weirdly wonderful? For instance:

- Try saying your name over and over again. Can you believe that's your name?!
- What little thing catches your attention, now that you're really looking?

Once you've discovered something in your life that you'd describe as "weirdly wonderful," move on to the Reflection Prompt, and then let the "for the day" practice lead you into delight as you cultivate a spirit of joy.

- *What did you experience that seemed weirdly wonderful?*
- *What allows for the unexpected to become wonderful as the experience continues?*

FOR THE DAY

- *On your 2nd to last celebration day, take some time to let something "weird" become wonderful. Pair something unusual with something familiar. Wear crazy socks. Mismatch your prints. Eat dessert first. Buy bedazzled reading glasses. Watch cat videos. Let the surprise and the amazingness of the world be your playground on this fine, weirdly wonderful day.*

WEEK 13

ABUNDANCE & FREEDOM

DAY 85: CREATING ABUNDANCE

What to bring to your practice: *Your environment and real life, Joy Journal (optional)*

Joyful abundance creates a sense of freedom
that allows the whole self to relax.

*W*elcome to this 13th and final week in our Joy Journey! Changes in our lives, like coming to the end of a journey like this one, can be both scary and exciting all at the same time. There isn't a specific practice and reflection prompt assigned to Day 91. But as you continue on into a new season of life, you will be equipped with numerous tools and resources to help you navigate the many twists and turns along the way. However, it's not over yet! Before you head off into whatever is next for you, we turn our attention to just one more theme: Abundance and Freedom.

Abundance turns out to be an amazingly important topic when it comes to joy because most of humanity knows all too well what it is like to live with the fear of not having enough. This fear is embedded deep within us, often triggering our flight, fright, freeze, or fawn reactions as we ask numerous questions relating to lack. Will we have enough time, money, energy, food, water…?

But the good news is, through our practices, we can offer ourselves little gifts of abundance on a regular basis, calming the lower part of the brain while bringing the parasympathetic parts of the brain back online. As we begin to feel calmer, logic and reason become more possible. A sense of freedom starts to emerge and Joy increases, even thrives.

Adding abundance to our lives can look like a lot of things, and we'll be exploring many of these themes throughout the week, but to get us started, we can:

DECLUTTER

- Delete, delegate or delay things and experiences that drain us of energy.
- Schedule breaks into our days
- Organize a space that is causing us stress

ADD COLOR, LIGHT, TEXTURE, LIFE, ETC.

- Add colorful pillows, blankets, or wall hangings
- Wear a fun color
- Hang up a string of lights
- Become a plant owner
- Add texture
- Stretch those muscles
- Schedule fun time, dates with friends, free nights, mini-vacations…

These are just a few ways to make abundance a regular practice in our lives, opening up our ability to experience more Joy. And so as we begin this final week, our spiritual practice for today is to literally make a plan to create abundance in our daily lives.

PRACTICE

Today we turn our attention towards *creating abundance in our day-to-day lives.*

And to help us get started, offer yourself a centering breath, begin to calm the body and the mind, and follow the reflection prompt below.

- *Where can I create abundance in my life today?*

When your practice is complete, if you'd like, close by offering yourself this closing blessing:

May I find the ability to choose joyful abundance in my heart, and in doing so, experience an increasing well of freedom so that I can live into Joy, the unlimited essence of my being.

DAY 86: SOUND BATHING

What to bring to your practice: *Joy Song, Joy Journal (optional)*
Also possible: *Google "5-minute sound bath" or find one at TendingMe.com*

At the heart of all things is pure Joy.

$\mathcal{A}$s we explore the theme of Abundance and Freedom this week, we turn our attention to calming the body through the practice of Sound Bathing.

For those who may not be familiar, sound bathing is the experience of being "bathed" in sound waves while allowing ourselves to let go of the usual treadmill experience of our own thoughts. Many find that sound is a useful catalyst for opening to the awareness of Presence. And from that space, connection to Joy can flow more naturally.

Note: Sound bathing is not recommended for anyone who has recently suffered a concussion. If you have not fully recovered from a concussion, an alternative to sound bathing could be to simply sit and be present to the sounds in your own backyard or local park. You may also want to check with a doctor if you are pregnant or have metal inside your body. If there is any question, always check with your doctor first.

PRACTICE

For those who are able, using either your Joy Song or a 5-minute audio clip of a Sound Bath, move to a comfortable sitting or lying down position. Begin by following the breath, and then allow yourself to become present to the sounds you hear.

As your practice comes to a close, pay attention to your overall being.

- *What do you feel?*
- *Is there anything you feel able to let go of, whether it be stress, thoughts, emotions, or something else?*
- *In what ways does stillness contribute to your connection to joy?*

DAY 87: ABUNDANCE IN NATURE

What to bring to your practice: *Your natural surroundings, Joy Journal (optional)*

FOUND IN TAITTIRIYA UPANISHAD
From Joy we have come,
In Joy we live and have our being, and
in that sacred Joy we will one day melt again.
—Translation, The Self-Realization Fellowship

*N*ature can be a place that offers us great feelings of liberation. It may be that being at the beach allows you to lay down your worries. Spending time among trees may give you a sense of rootedness. Blooming flowers may ignite your sense of being alive.

As we learned on Day 86, spending time in a meaningfully sensory-rich environment can help us move from spaces of alarm to spaces of peace. And as it turns out, our natural environment is incredibly sensory rich!

The sun provides light, but the light is ever-changing as clouds move throughout the sky. Early summer days may offer us the smell of fresh lilacs but come fall, fresh fallen leaves fill our noses instead. Many of us may easily call to mind the smell of rain, freshly mowed lawn… And if all of that weren't enough, there is the tapestry of colors. If we sit and really look, we soon begin to see there is not just one shade of green, brown, blue, pink, or any other color. Even the feeling of the air can shift as we move closer or farther away from water, or from the cover of a shaded tree out into the open. Being in nature offers freedom to our senses.

And so today's spiritual practice leads us outdoors.

PRACTICE

Allow nature to show you the joy of abundance by way of your senses, paying special attention to any connections you become aware of.

And when your practice is complete:

- *What joy emerges as you take in your natural surroundings?*

DAY 88: BLUE MIND

What to bring to your practice: *Water, Joy Journal*

A joyful life is one that includes space for the things that matter to you.

Many Indigenous people believe that not only is water life, but that water is also alive, listening to us. Water connects us all, not only through space, but also through time. Whether we are alive now or were alive many years ago, water has been there for us and with us.

WHAT IS BLUE MIND?

In some circles, people refer to these states of mind we've been talking about this week using color designations. The fearful mind would be described as Red Mind while a calm and peaceful mind would be described as Blue Mind.

Many have found that spending contemplative time with water in any way—drinking a glass of water, taking a shower, sitting near a body of water, even sitting near a fish tank—can create this calmer state in us from which Joy can flow.

And so our Spiritual Practice for today involves *engaging our Blue Mind.*

PRACTICE

- Begin by situating yourself near water. If at all possible, allowing your body to actually feel the water may aid your sensory experience. But again, even just slowly drinking a glass of water can be meaningful.
- As you begin to sit in this contemplative space, if you have questions or prayers, allow these to emerge during this time. Don't worry about solving them. But just as we would light a candle to signify Presence, so it is with water. To be contemplative is to become aware of Divine Presence.
- As you sit, breathing mindfully for a couple of moments, you may find thoughts arising, maybe even possible solutions coming to the fore or tasks trying to move you along. If the thought seems important, allow yourself to make a note of it but then return again to simply being in Presence. In thinking about our opening words for today, the calm space you are curating for yourself right now is one of those things that matters.

- *For your reflection: What emerged for you today in this "blue mind" environment?*
- *How does it help (or not help) you make space in your life?*

DAY 89: FOREST BATHING

What to bring to your practice: *Your natural environment, Joy Journal*

When we open our awareness,
taking note of all the wonderful things around us,
we increase our sense of abundance.

$\mathcal{I}$n 1982, the Japanese government coined the term *shinrin-yoku,* translated as *forest bathing.* In 1984, biologist E.O. Wilson coined the term *biophilia,* showing us that experiences with plants and animals are an essential part of our well-being, that we are naturally attracted to other living things.

Forest bathing, simply put, is "bathing," or "immersing oneself" in a forest atmosphere. That being said, many have been quick to mention that a forest is not necessary. Natural green spaces of any kind will do, though the presence of trees is highly recommended.

Whatever natural environment one has access to, the goal of forest bathing is straightforward:

- To live in the present moment while immersing our senses in the sights and sounds of a natural setting, all the while moving slowly.

Even just 5 minutes in nature improves wellness in a whole myriad of ways—mental, physical, emotional, and spiritual. So our spiritual practice for today—on this penultimate day of our journey—is to once again take our practice outdoors, this time for our own mini-experience of forest bathing:

PRACTICE

Forest bathing offers the opportunity to:

- Breathe mindfully
- Walk slowly
- Use your senses in nature, paying attention to:
  - Sensations in your body
  - Sights you see
  - Scents you smell
  - Things you hear

- *Offer yourself 5 to 10 minutes in nature, focusing on one or more of the options above.*

- *For your reflection: In what ways did abundance and freedom become apparent to you?*
- *In what ways did you receive access to Joy?*

DAY 90: JOY IN US!

What to bring to your practice: *Joy Journal*

Joy resides within, not "out there," but "in here."

*J*oy-Journeyer, you have done it! For 90 days you have engaged in spiritual practices, investing yourself daily in order to increase your quality of life from a joy perspective. Wow! Today is a very big day for you. From here you will continue your journey, returning whenever you'd like to the tools and practices that you've acquired along the way.

PRACTICE

The haiku below offers us a chance to reflect on what we've been up to in these past 90 days. In that slow and contemplative way we've been practicing, give yourself time with the words. Take a centering breath, read it a couple of times, including at least one time out loud:

PURE LOVE, JOY, AND LIGHT
Why do I insist
That my worth should be measured
By numbered results

I'm not only this
There's another part of me
Pure love, joy, and light
—August 2022

- *As you pause to reflect on the words above, you may wish to ask yourself: What do I want to take with me from this journey?*

BLESSING

*I*n this moment, as you cross over the threshold into that which comes next for you, I offer you a blessing that you have offered to others many times during these 90 days:

May you be well!

I feel incredibly blessed that you have said yes to taking this journey with me. Thank you for investing in you. I pray that all we've shared together will produce fruit in your life for years to come. May you always remember that the Joy you seek resides within you as the unlimited essence of your being.

APPENDIX A

CELEBRATION WORKSHEET

SIX THINGS THAT CAUSE ME TO SMILE

1. _____
2. _____
3. _____
4. _____
5. _____
6. _____

MY SENSES LISTS

Taste

1. _____
2. _____
3. _____
4. _____

Smell

1. _____
2. _____
3. _____
4. _____

Feel

1. _____
2. _____
3. _____
4. _____

Sight

1. _____
2. _____
3. _____
4. _____

Sound

1. _____
2. _____
3. _____
4. _____

TWO TIMES OF DAY WHEN CELEBRATION WOULD BE POSSIBLE FOR ME

1. _____
2. _____

TWO PEOPLE WHO COULD HELP ME CELEBRATE

1. _____
2. _____

APPENDIX B

MORE ABOUT KRISTINA'S JOURNEY

This 90-Day Journey came into being by way of both research and personal experience. It was important to me to write only what I knew, only what I had experienced myself. In the introduction, you were asked to choose at least one song that would become your Joy Song. On my own journey, I had something of a playlist. Below, I'm sharing some of my favorites with you.

SONGS FOUND ON YOUTUBE

Collins, J. *Generosity*.
https://www.youtube.com/watch?v=nF3yJg45NZY

Elise, L., Awosika, A., Pollock, B., Lawrence, J., Conner, J. *Mantragold - Gratitude*. https://www.youtube.com/watch?v=u60RnlO7-xQ

Jones, S. *Meditation on Breathing*.

https://www.youtube.com/watch?v=YHHxeDludT4

Kool & the Gang. 1980. *Celebration*.
https://www.youtube.com/watch?v=3GwjfUFyY6M

Kowalski, T. *Luminescence*.
https://www.youtube.com/watch?v=LsS_fVOmuKM

Levine, B. *We Rise*.
https://www.youtube.com/watch?v=5PxuNO7bc6k

Patel, N., Nahmod, D. *Grateful: A Love Song to the World*.
https://www.youtube.com/watch?v=sO2o98Zpzg8

Sarton, A. *Joy*. Recorded by Beautiful Chorus.
https://www.youtube.com/watch?v=ySzm_3t6ocU

Sarton, A. *Heart Chakra*. Recorded by Beautiful Chorus.
https://www.youtube.com/watch?v=g4IZrY9lirI

Timberlake, J. *Can't Stop the Feeling*.
https://www.youtube.com/watch?v=ru0K8uYEZWw

SOCIAL MEDIA VIDEOS

DeLeo, L. *Laughter Yoga. TEDX Montreal Women*.
https://www.youtube.com/watch?v=4p4dZ0afivk

Uplift. *Speaking to the Water with Pat McCabe*.
https://www.youtube.com/watch?v=OeeAMNxuqio

POETRY BOOKS

Cole-Dai, P., Wilson, R. *Poetry of Presence: An Anthology of Mindfulness*

Poems. Grayson Books, 2017.

Harkin, C. *Let Us Dance!: The Stumble and Whirl with the Beloved.* Self-published, 2021.

Harkin, C. *Susceptible to Light.* Soulfruit Publishing, 2020.

Norris, G. *Being Home: Discovering the Spiritual in the Everyday.* Hidden Spring, 2002.

Roberts, E.; Amidon, E., eds. *Earth Prayers: 365 Prayers, Poems, and Invocations from Around the World.* Harper One, 2009.

BIBLIOGRAPHY

ARTICLES

Brower, T. "Purpose May Be the Key to Happiness: 3 Reasons Why." *Forbes,* March 19, 2023. https://www.forbes.com/sites/tracybrower/2023/03/19/purpose-may-be-the-key-to-happiness-3-reasons-why/?sh=5cfb4ba15427

Brussat, F., Brussat, M. "Letting Go." *Spirituality & Practice.* (No date.) https://www.spiritualityandpractice.com/practices/features/view/18407

Das, S. "The Mysticism of Rabindranath Tagore: What Tagore's Poetry Teaches Us About God." *Learn Religions.* January 29, 2019. https://www.learnreligions.com/the-mysticism-of-rabindranath-tagore-1770325

Holder, M. "Measuring Happiness: How Can We Measure It?" *Psychology Today.* May 22, 2017. https://www.psychologytoday.com/us/blog/the-happiness-doctor/201705/measuring-happiness-how-can-we-measure-it

Intermountain Health. "The Health Benefits of Smiling." June, 2019. https://www.sclhealth.org/blog/2019/06/the-real-health-benefits-of-smiling-and-laughing/

Loadman-Copeland, Kirk. "Joy: Introduction to the Theme." *Touchstones Project: A Monthly Journal of Unitarian Universalism*, 1:6; 2022. https://www.touchstonesproject.com/_files/ugd/552cc1_3a47893433624122b2a19b461b97fa74.pdf

Muller, R. "14 People on the Moment of Kindness that Changed their Lives." *Shine.* December 4, 2018. https://advice.theshineapp.com/articles/14-people-on-the-moment-of-kindness-that-changed-their-lives/

National Institute for Play. "What Are Your Play Personalities?" (No date.) https://www.nifplay.org/what-is-play/play-personalities/

Paes, T. "Creativity and Pretend Play." *British Council.* (No date.) https://www.britishcouncil.org/programmes/creative-play/creativity-pretend-play

Palmer, J. "The Ten Thousand Joys and Ten Thousand Sorrows." 2019. https://www.jimpalmerauthor.com/post/the-ten-thousand-joys-and-ten-thousand-sorrows

Salzberg, S. "Becoming the Ally of All Beings." *Lion's Roar.* (No date.) https://www.lionsroar.com/becoming-the-ally-of-all-beings/

Taylor, S. "7 Benefits of Gratitude." *Wellness Matters.* November 23, 2019. https://www.conehealth.com/services/behavioral-health/outpatient-behavioral-health-care/7-benefits-of-gratitude/

The Little Gym. "The Importance of Creative Play for Kids" [Blog]. (No date.) https://www.thelittlegym.com/blog/2017/9/the-importance-of-creative-play-for-kids

Trinity Family Wealth Advisors. "The 7 Forms of Generosity" [Blog]. (No date.) https://trinityfamilywealth.ca/the-7-forms-of-generosity-2/

Wade, D., Des Marais, S. "The Importance of Play for Adults." *Psych Central* [Blog]. (No date.) https://psychcentral.com/blog/the-importance-of-play-for-adults#how-to-be-more-playful

Willard, C. "6 Ways to Enjoy Mindful Walking." *Mindful.* December 15, 2020. https://www.mindful.org/6-ways-to-get-the-benefits-of-mindful-walking/

BOOKS

Beck, Martha. *The Joy Diet: Ten Daily Practices for a Happier Life.* Crown Publishers, 2003.

Cope, S. *The Great Work of Your Life: A Guide for the Journey to Your True Calling.* Bantam Books, 2012.

Goff-Maidoff, I. *The Joy Book: Celebrating the Presence and the Practice of Joy.* Sarah's Circle Publishing, 2008.

Hendricks, G. *The Big Leap: Conquer Your Hidden Fear and Take Life to the Next Level.* Harper One, 2010.

Holmes, Barbara A. *Joy Unspeakable: Contemplative Practices of the Black Church* (2nd ed.). Fortress Press, 2017.

Kaur, V. *See No Stranger: A Memoir and Manifesto of Revolutionary Love.* One World, 2020.

Lama, His Holiness D., Tutu, Archbishop D., Abrams, D. *The Book of Joy: Lasting Happiness in a Changing World.* Penguin, 2016.

Lee, Ingrid Fetell. *Joyful: The Surprising Power of Ordinary Things to Create Extraordinary Happiness.* Hachette Book Group, 2018.

VIDEOS & FILMS

Bertin, M. A Daily Mindful Walking Practice. *Mindful.* 2017. https://www.mindful.org/daily-mindful-walking-practice/

Kaiser, Kristina. *Joie de Vivre Journey: Twenty Short Videos for Bringing More Joy.* 2021. https://www.youtube.com/playlist?list=PLqHSsdbdc-0lz92aLEhjojkz-ohkNnywy

Lama, His Holiness D., Curry, Bishop M., Zaki, J., Coan, J., Wilson, R., Donovan, C., Salbi, Z. *Global Joy Summit: A 4-Day Celebration and Exploration of Living with Joy in Challenging Times.* 2022. https://www.globaljoysummit.org/summit-home#still-available

Psihoyos, L. (Director), Callahan, P. (Co-Director). *Mission: Joy—Finding Happiness in Troubled Times* [Film]. Voices4Freedom, The Film Collaborative, MORE, 2021.

Sinek. S. *Generosity Kindness Gratitude & Oxytocin.* June 9, 2021. https://www.youtube.com/watch?v=IwmpUb006O4

Made in the USA
Coppell, TX
11 February 2025